D1383033

RETIREMENT

New Beginnings
New Challenges
New Successes

LEO HAUSER & VINCENT A. MILLER

RETIREMENT

**New Beginnings
New Challenges
New Successes**

FIVE STEPS TO THE BEST YEARS OF YOUR LIFE

Retirement: New Beginnings, New Challenges, New Successes.
Copyright © 1989 by Leo Hauser, Vincent A. Miller

Library of Congress Cataloging-in-Publication Data

Hauser, Leo
    Retirement: new beginnings, new challenges, new successes.

    1. Retirement—United States. 2. Self-actualization
(Psychology) 3. Aging—United States—Psychological aspects.
I. Miller, Vincent A.   II. Title
HQ1062.H34   1989   646.7'9   89-1455
ISBN 0-937721-59-X

Edited by: Donna Hoel
Design & Production: Wenda Johnson
Printed in the United States of America

10 9 8 7 6 5 4 3 2 1

Published by:

DCI Publishing, Inc.
P.O. Box 379
Wayzata, MN 55391

CONTENTS

STEP TWO:

STEP THREE:

DEDICATION

This book is dedicated to the spouses of newly retired persons whose lives are sometimes changed by retirement as much as the life of the person who retires. We hope this book will ease the conflict that occurs when the newly retired person becomes a "couch potato." The person who follows the *Five Steps to the Best Years of Your Life* will adapt to the new lifestyle of retirement and will keep family life in proper perspective.

PREFACE

We don't want to confuse you, so we'd better state right off that, although this book is co-authored, most of it is written as if just one person was speaking to you. There's a reason for that. We, the authors, want to talk to you directly. We think what we have to say will be more effective that way.

We don't think our method of presentation will be confusing to you. We do know that both of us were in such complete and total agreement about everything that went into the creation of this book, it doesn't matter *who* wrote it.

We've worked hard to keep this book short, simple, to the point, and easy to read. We like to meet issues head-on, make necessary decisions, and move into action. We assume you do too.

We think you should know something about the background of your authors, other than what you will read in the book. Both of us have been involved in training and human resource development for many years. Vince Miller was President of the American Society for Training and Development in 1974. He was Secretary-Treasurer for the International Federation of Training and Development Organizations in 1973 and 1974. He is the author of the *Guidebook for International Trainers in Business and Industry*. He has been retired since January 1983.

Leo Hauser was also President of the American Society for Training and Development—in 1976. He was President of the International Federation of Training and Development Organizations in 1978. Leo is the author of a book titled *Five Steps to Success,* now in its sixth printing. He has reached a reasonable retirement age but has chosen not to retire.

So, as Joan Rivers would say, "Now, can we talk?"

We, the authors, bring to you a wealth of experience. We'll be telling you about our experiences in sales and marketing, on the New York Stock Exchange, in industry, and with our world-wide training networks. We know whereof we speak—from our personal experiences and from our training contacts. We'll talk about your retirement needs.

You might wonder how we, the authors, came together in this joint effort. It all started from a conversation at the national conference of the American Society for Training and Development.

When the subject of retirement training came up, we agreed there were many pre-retirement training programs, but neither of us could identify a post-retirement training program.

We went farther. While still at the conference, we checked for post-retirement programs through computers that were tied into national information mainframes and the Library of Congress.

We didn't find anything that will compare with what we're producing here. We believe you will appreciate our help, and we're ready to start right now.

Leo Hauser and Vincent A. Miller

RETIREMENT: NEW BEGINNINGS, NEW CHALLENGES

PROLOGUE

GETTING READY TO MARCH ON OUT

One-third of your life. If we told you it was yours to do whatever you wanted, what would you think? The scoffers might say, "That'll be the day!" Others might respond, "Tell me more!"

Well, as of 1990, one-third of a lifetime will be available to many folks—as retirement. We're living longer, healthier lives, and a 90+ lifespan will be a reality for a good number of us. Think about it. Two-thirds of all the men and women who have ever, *in the entire history of the world,* reached age 65 are alive right at this very moment!

In the USA, about 5,000 people retire every day. That's getting close to two million people a year. And the numbers are growing. In the past 20 years, the

1

over-65 age group has grown more than twice as fast as the rest of the population. Looking at the entire twentieth century, the American population has increased five times—but the over-65ers have increased by nearly 13 times. In 1983, the 65 and older group passed up the teenagers. Some experts predict, with continuing improvements in health and fitness, by the year 2000 close to 20 percent of our nation will be over age 65. That's one in every five people!

This whole idea of long healthy retirements is brand new. Most people have been conditioned to think of retirement as a point close to the end of the downhill stretch that begins around age 40. Not true! We need to think of life as an exciting *ascension*—a continuous rise with new challenges and opportunities. And that's where this book is going to help you.

Once Again, Be Prepared!

Most of us spent the first quarter century or so of our lives preparing for the second quarter century. It stands to reason we should set aside part of our present time to think about the next quarter century. What if we do have another good, healthy 25 or 30 years ahead? What do we really want to do with them?

We tease and joke about being "out to pasture." We look forward to the end of the "rat race." We anticipate retirement as our time for freedom and control. But do we really want to retire?

Retire. It's an interesting word—with some surprising meanings. It can mean "retreat," "withdraw," "recede," or "to put out" (as to retire a side in baseball). It almost feels inappropriate to use that same word to describe the end of a particular occupation or profession. It feels like such a negative word for what should be such a positive experience.

One definition we do like is "to win possession of" as in to retire a trophy or an athlete's team number. That's what we'd like to teach you to do—to win possession of your own skills and talents and use them to make your older years happy and fulfilling.

Are You an Uncle Charlie?

You probably have or know an "Uncle Charlie." Our typical Uncle Charlie worked in industry all his life, never married, never cultivated any hobbies. He *lived* to retire! When that day finally came, he packed up his car (which he now referred to as his "rig") and headed west to see a world he had only imagined through reading and television.

No doubt he landed at your door somewhere along the way, looking lonely and perhaps a little confused—much older than he should at a mere 65. He tried to sound enthusiastic as he talked about his new freedom, but the words were hollow. He had already been on the road two months, had spent as much time as he comfortably could with friends and relatives. Where was all the fun and adventure he had so looked forward to?

Maybe he stayed with you a while. Probably he made you feel kind of guilty because you couldn't take much time from your busy schedule to show him around. Eventually he left. And six months later you heard he died—alone, back home. He just went to sleep and didn't wake up. What went wrong?

Surely Uncle Charlie had a plan. He wanted to travel, to see the country he held so dear. But could it be that wasn't enough? Did he need more to make life worth living?

Now, we didn't tell that story to scare anybody. Even though you've heard many anecdotes to the contrary, most people don't die soon after retirement. In fact, the most recent information supports your insurance company's claim that health usually improves after retirement. If you're forced to retire because of health, retirement isn't necessarily going to make you better. But if retirement brings a release from stress and pressures, chances are you may feel years younger in just a few weeks.

But there's still that nagging question of the purpose and value of older people in our society. Just living longer isn't in everyone's best interest. It's living well—physically, mentally, and spiritually—that gets us excited about facing new challenges.

Would You Rather Be a Bud?

We're reminded of our friend and neighbor, Bud, who sold his business and retired at age 82. He then began tackling those tasks he had put off for so long. He painted the house, inside and out, twice! He drove to Arizona and back and to California and back, twice! After two short years, he had had enough "leisure."

Bud knew a company he had stock in was struggling. "The young fellas [45 and 50 years old!] know how to sell, but they haven't had time to learn to run a company," he told us. "I think I better give them a hand."

So he did. He turned the operation around and once again felt good about his life. Now, lest you think Bud doesn't know how to enjoy anything but work, we'll tell you more. Among other hobbies, Bud enjoys singing. In fact, he has sung in a community chorus—for 63 years! The group is excellent and travels extensively, even competing internationally. (A few years ago, they won second place—"*The Silver*," as Bud says—in the International Choral "Olympics" in Wales.) Before competitions, the chorus rehearses four or five nights a week. And all the music is memorized!

One Saturday afternoon, just before a recent trip to a music festival in France, Bud did call to say he would be late for rehearsal. He was at the plant helping unload an important shipment of goods!! After all, he's only 88 years old!

Incidentally, Bud is planning on being around for a while yet. In fact, he's decided he probably should build a new house. The elegant "executive" homes around him, all built on land Bud only recently sold, are making his house look a bit modest. But you can bet he has a healthy bank account as a result of the land sales.

The Parade's About to Begin

Study after study has shown that the people who are happiest in retirement are those with busy, productive lives. They are "givers," with strong needs to give back to society part of what has been given them. They seem to be involved in everything—volunteering, calling on friends, working, and yes, even making money.

Money does seem to be a major factor in staying vigorous in our mature years. The Social Security Administration reports that among every 100 people who retire, 95 need their Social Security just to stay above water. Of the other five, two inherited wealth and three made enough money on their own. Surely most of us want more than just to keep our heads above water. But what are we to do?

The next 100 or so pages are going to give you lots of ideas about what you are to do. And that's the key. You must *do* something. The fact you even picked up this book is a positive sign you're on track. So read on, and we'll share some exciting ideas for making sure the best is yet to come.

Get Yourself into This Picture

Now it's time for *you* to enter our scenario. Imagine yourself as having been retired for some time. The backyard fence is repaired. The basement is spick and span. You don't want to play golf every day of the week. Life is getting to be a little dull, tedious, and boring, and your spouse is urging you to get up out of that easy chair and get some exercise.

Or maybe you've moved into your retirement condominium, and life is just not as exciting as you thought it would be. There is no lawn to mow and no repairs to make on the house. You and your spouse are in smaller quarters, and you're getting on each other's nerves. Things are just not like they were before you retired. There is no one to boss around, no one to type your letters. About the best service you can get out of your old office when you drop by to chat is free use of the copy machine. Everybody seems too busy.

Maybe you retired early on one of those blue light specials so many companies are offering their older employees, but you're too young to be totally retired.

Whatever the circumstances: Don't just sit there. Do something! I can remember my sports coach in high school yelling that at me as I should have been fighting for the ball. "Don't just stand there! Do something!" Those were the words the foreman used as I worked on my first production line job during the big depression. Jobs were scarce, and the foreman felt justified driving his workers to get maximum production from them. "Don't just stand there! Do something!" is our message to you as you retire from a lifetime of work.

My father's experience is one of the horrible examples of what can happen to a person who has no outside interests and no involvement after retirement. He was robust and healthy when he retired at 68 years of age. But he had no outside interests, so he did a lot of sitting and watching television. His body functions slowed down. His speech became slower. Even his thought processes were slower. Within a year, he was a semi-invalid and had aged immeasurably. I blamed it all on his just giving up and treating retirement as if it were the end of the road. I should have said to my father, "Don't just sit there! Do something!" But, since he was my father, I respectfully kept my mouth shut.

Fortunately, this story has a happy ending. After eight years, a doctor discovered there was a medical reason for some of my dad's slow body functions. With medical treatment, his sharp wit returned, his body became stronger, and he lived to be 92 years old.

We don't want you to get the feeling we're trying to scare you into doing something positive about your retirement life. It's true that a person who just "sits" will probably develop some health problems. Also, people who are bored, lonely, and don't have much physical activity in their lives have a tendency to depend on alcohol and drugs for their "kicks". But, enough of that. Let's look at some of the positive things that can happen to you after you reach retirement age.

Perhaps you know the story of Colonel Harland Sanders. There was some mention made of it in Leo Hauser's *Five Steps to Success*. The story is even more appropriate, now that we're talking about success after retirement.

Colonel Sanders was three years younger than my father, and his crisis in life came one year later, in 1956, at the age of 66. The Colonel's reaction to what amounted to a forced retirement was quite different from my father's. After age 66, Colonel Sanders became one of the most recognized men on earth, and in doing so, he amassed a fortune. That's what makes the Colonel's story so appropriate to tell at this time.

As noted in *The Five Steps To Success*, the Colonel had worked for years to build a thriving business. By 1953, Sander's Cafe was valued at $165,000, and he was looking forward, with savings and Social Security, to a comfortable retirement sometime in the future. But, things do change. The highway on which his restaurant was located was rerouted. This literally put him out of business. Three years later, in 1956, he was forced to sell everything at auction to cover his debts. But, even at age 66, the Colonel was not ready to give up and retire on government hand-outs.

He remembered some of the publicity he had received from Duncan Hines in his "Adventures in Good Eating." He also remembered he had sold his recipe to a restaurant in 1952, and that restaurant had done very well with it. Also, several other restaurant owners had agreed to pay the Colonel four cents for every chicken they fried using his recipe.

So, he packed up his old 1946 Ford, grabbed his beloved pressure cooker and 50 pounds of his special (now famous) seasoning, with its secret herbs and spices, and began his tireless journey from restaurant to restaurant.

The Colonel talked to owners, chefs, and anyone else who would listen to him. He would offer to cook up a batch of chicken for the manager and employees and get them to agree that it was "finger-lickin' good." Then, he would offer to sell them his special seasoning and stay with them a few days to teach them his unusual cooking method.

It was during these early days that Colonel Sanders began to wear the white suit, white shirt, black string tie, black shoes, white moustache and goatee and to carry a cane. This Southern gentleman image—and his honorary Colonel's title—helped him promote his Kentucky Fried Chicken all over the world.

During the first two years, Colonel Sanders sold a total of five franchises. By 1960, two years later, he had sold 200 franchises. (Remember he was 70 years old in 1960.) By 1964, he had sold more than 800 franchises. That was when he sold the business for $2 million, plus a substantial yearly lifetime salary. The Colonel died at age 90.

In eight years, at an age when most people are content to think of retirement, the Colonel faced up to a situation and parlayed what he could do best into millions of dollars and introduced his "finger-lickin good" chicken to people all over the world. All of us have something we do best, and that talent in many cases has no connection with what we did when we were "working". We usually get a lot of pleasure out of doing what we do best. One thing we should consider, then, is what part that talent should play in our retirement life.

Let's set the record straight. You don't have to make a millions dollars after retirement from your regular job in order to have a successful and productive retirement. You may choose to do something that will net absolutely no income—and still have ample satisfaction in a job well done. The trick is to keep your body and mind active.

Making a Life

Psychiatrists often remind us we're taught how to make a living, but not how to make a life. That's especially true of the life after retirement. If we're lucky we may get some pre-retirement training, but that training only gets us ready for retirement. What do we do when retirement becomes a reality?

I'm reminded of my fellow worker, Ben, who thought he would be busy for months—maybe years—fixing his fence, cleaning his basement, and doing chores around the house. Two weeks after Ben retired, he was in the office telling us he had done everything he planned to do and was already bored with retirement.

Ben realized earlier than most that physical and mental activity cannot stop at retirement. He let everybody know he was bored and needed something to do. Ben had somehow stumbled on a part of the formula for having a successful and productive retirement. He knew he needed to keep busy, and he let everybody know he needed to do something to improve his retirement life. He soon had a full and busy life, including some volunteer work that gave satisfaction from helping others and a part-time job that supplemented his income.

It takes some people many months to realize they're wasting their retirement life. Some people never come face-to-face with reality. We can help you, but first you need to know yourself. Are you ready? Let's begin step one of your journey to a successful and productive retirement.

S^{TEP} O^{NE}

GET TO KNOW YOURSELF

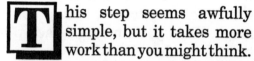

This step seems awfully simple, but it takes more work than you might think. Retirement means different things to different people. You'll have to be perfectly honest with yourself and decide what sort of retirement you want. We can guide you. We can give you the formula, but the end result will be all yours. Your chance for a successful retirement will be just as good as you are honest with yourself.

We want you to take an honest-to-goodness, objective look at yourself. Look back on your life and identify all those things you liked to do, especially the things you were good at and got results from. Then look back at the things you didn't like to do. Your experience will probably show that those things you disliked didn't work out so well for you.

The comparison between things you liked to do and things you didn't like is important. Before you retired, you probably had to do many things on your job that you didn't like. Chances are you didn't do them nearly as well as the things you liked to do. Now that you're retired, there is no reason why you should have to do something you dislike. At least, with proper planning, it can be your choice. The fact you made the choice will soften the pain if you do something you dislike.

Perhaps you've already heard the story about a good friend of mine, Jim Kaat. He's one of baseball's all time great left-handed pitchers. Jim was pitching for the Minnesota Twins in 1966 when the Twins acquired a new pitching coach named Johnny Sain.

Sain spent the first few days of spring training just watching his pitchers, taking notes, and not saying much. Finally, Sain called each pitcher in, one at a time, for a chat.

When his turn came to meet with Johnny Sain, Jim Kaat figured Sain would have some profound advice. He'd been working like the devil on his full repertoire of pitches and was ready to learn from his new coach.

Jim," said Sain, "of your four best pitches, which one is best?"

Jim had been doing his homework. He'd been studying the effectiveness of his pitches, and he could name the best one right off.

"My best pitch is my fastball. Then comes my curve. Next is my slider and finally, my change-up."

"What have you been working on this week?" asked Sain.

"My slider and my change up," said Jim. "If I can improve on those two pitches, I know I'll have a good season."

Sain looked at Jim for a minute and then shook his head.

"I don't see it that way, Jim. I'd like you to take a different approach. Your fastball is your best pitch. I want you to go out there in practice, warm-ups, and games and concentrate on your fastball. I want to see you throwing your fastball 80 to 90 percent of the time, all year, in every game. Do that, and you'll win a lot of ballgames."

Jim was stunned. It wasn't what he had expected at all. He thought he'd get some technical advice about improving his curve, or cleaning up his slider. But instead, Sain had told him to go out and do more of what he already did best.

Jim wasn't one to argue with his coach, especially one with a reputation like Johnny Sain's. As Jim tells it, "I saluted, clicked my heels, said 'Yes, Sir', and went out and pitched fastballs like you never saw. I threw so many fastballs I thought my arm was going to fall off."

But Jim's arm didn't fall off. And in that year he went on to win 26 games and become pitcher of the year in the American League.

Now, let me ask you the $64,000 question. **Do you know what your fastball is?** Do you even know what your best pitch is? If you do, have you been throwing it 80 to 90 percent of the time? Or are you spending your time in mediocrity by letting your God-given strengths and talents sit idle?

You have complete charge of your retirement life. It's not like your work life, where the boss or the job description dictated what you were to do. Now, it's *your* choice.

So how do you go about finding your fastball? The first thing you have to do is get to know yourself. Now that sounds pretty simple, doesn't it? If you are like me, your first response might be something like this.

"Hey, I know who I am. I'm Leo Hauser from Wayzata, Minnesota. I'm six feet, two inches tall, have brown hair and brown eyes, and look pretty good if I say so myself. Yeah, that's me. I'm the same guy who shaved himself this morning and the morning before that."

But you also know what we're really talking about is looking at your repertoire of pitches (your positive success attributes) the way Jim Kaat did and finding your fastball. And while you're searching for your fastball, you'll have to decide what pitches you want to use in your retirement and how you want to use them.

Let's look at it this way. You've been planting and cultivating a flower garden all your life. Now it's time to smell the roses. You can sell some of them. You can give some away, but for your own sake don't let the flowers die without doing something with them. Your successful and productive retirement depends on your ability to satisfy your own needs as well as the needs of others. And to the extent you give others what they want, they in return will give you the goods, services, emotional satisfaction, and positive results you want and enjoy.

Treating Yourself as a Business

I overheard one retiree telling another: "I woke up this morning and didn't have anything to do. And now it's evening and I'm only half done."

I hope he was kidding. I can't imagine anything worse than waking up and not having anything to do. I thank God every morning when I get up that I have something to do that must be done.

Now, I don't think you should be overburdened with work in your retirement, and I don't think everything you do should be work. What I'm trying to say is, now that you're retired, you have more control over your life and should plan it to be interesting, enjoyable, and productive. You might find this hard to believe, but it's true. You should start treating yourself as a business.

What is it that companies like McDonalds or Kentucky Fried Chicken do before they locate in a new town or a new section of town? They do a market survey. They determine their potential on the basis of population, individual income, size of the territory, age mix of the population, past performance under similar market conditions, and many other factors too numerous to mention.

Now, if you treat yourself, and your retirement, like a business, you'll want to do a market survey. You'll want to look at your working life and your hobbies. You'll want to look at your financial needs and what it is that gives you the most pleasure in your life. You'll have to look at what you do best and how you can transfer your work skills or your hobbies into something you want to do in your retirement. If you're planning new hobbies, you'll have to look at the cost and see if your budget can support the new hobbies.

Taking a Personal Inventory

The first thing you have to do is take a personal inventory. We're not talking about money now. We want you to figure out what you have to work with. What are your life experiences? How can you apply them to benefit you and other people in your retirement? You've got to take stock of what you have to work with in order to get a good return on your investment of time and effort in your retirement.

Honesty is what makes this exercise work. And sometimes honesty is hard to come by. None of us likes to look in the mirror and admit the face looking back has some imperfections.

But chances are if you look at yourself in the mirror critically you will see a few wrinkles—and maybe some gray hair you wish you didn't have. What we want to do in this personal inventory is to look at your warts and wrinkles as well as at your wonderfulness. You're not going to write a piece of campaign propaganda or try to sell yourself to someone else. You're going to establish the foundation for your future.

Our approach to completing a personal strengths inventory isn't original with us. It was invented by B. Franklin, printer. That's right. Benjamin Franklin, creator of the lightning rod, the postoffice, and the lending library, is the author of America's first inspirational self-help book. And he invented a sure-fire stock-taking technique.

"There is no problem," said Franklin, "that cannot be solved with a pad of paper and a pen." If Franklin had lived to see the automobile, television, and stereo hi-fi, he might have added a third element; a quiet place to think.

The Franklin/Hauser stock-taking system goes like this:

Concentration

Get away. Go someplace where you can be alone and concentrate on your strengths and weaknesses. Get off by yourself. Go to a park, or get in a canoe and paddle out into the middle of the lake, or go to the public library where you can expect it to be quiet.

Be sure to take along a pad of paper, a pen or pencil, and this book. You might want to refer to something written in the book, and you might want to do your planning on the pages provided in this book, although you probably will need additional pages if you do a thorough job. If you page forward several pages, you'll see that we will first be working with Worksheet Number 1 and Worksheet Number 2.

Be Objective

If you're using paper instead of the book, draw a line down the center of the page. Or you can just copy the wording shown on Worksheet Number 1 in this book. If so, put the following words on one side of the line.

> ### Strengths: Talents, Abilities, and Things I Like to Do.

On the other side of the line, write the words shown on Worksheet Number 2.

> ### Weaknesses: Things I'm Not Very Good At and Don't Like to Do.

Terrific and Like

Now that you have your paper set up, work on the first side of the sheet. Write down those things you're good at. Don't limit yourself to the things you did at work. Don't put things down because you think other people want you to. Don't put down things you find hard to do. If they're hard, they can probably be counted as weaknesses rather than strengths.

List the things that are easy and fun. List the hobbies you never thought of as work. If babysitting is a blast for you, write it down. If you enjoy photography, write it down. If barbecuing is your thing and everyone raves about your Fourth of July sauce, put it down. Remember the Colonel. Your barbecue sauce could possibly provide some of your retirement income and pleasure.

If you have a home computer and really enjoy working on it, write it down. The possibilities for turning your computer skills into a profit-making or pleasurable volunteer venture boggle the mind.

You get the gist of what you should do with Worksheet Number 1. You'll really be surprised at the long list of strengths, abilities, and things you like to do—provided you've done some soul searching and are honest with yourself. Spend plenty of time on this worksheet. It will probably be the most important decision-making tool you will use as you work toward a successful and productive retirement.

Lousy and Dislike

Lousy and Dislike is another label for Worksheet Number 2, which we've more elegantly called: Weaknesses: Things I'm not very good at and don't like to do.

Don't be surprised if you find it easier to write this list than the "strengths" list. You've spent most of your life learning to criticize yourself and others. At school, at work, in fact everywhere, it's the same story. Our whole culture is preoccupied with criticism. Sometimes we call it by different names, such as appraisal or evaluation, but it's all the same.

Lot of people think of themselves as complete klutzes. Turn on your television and what do you see? Commercials telling you how bad you smell, look, and feel. So, don't be surprised if after you've made your two lists you have five or six times as many bad traits and dislikes as good ones and likes.

Appraisal Time

Now it's time to narrow your list of attributes, talents, and skills to one or two things you're legitimately good at and like to do. In other words, look for one or two items on your list that have earned you the applause of others in some way. These are the things you'd do whether you had to or not, even if nobody applauded. They're the talents you want to concentrate on—especially if you want to turn your retirement into a profitable or pleasureable venture. Don't let go of the top one or two items on your list. This is the key to your retirement future. *This is your fastball.*

Now, let's remember our main objective is for you to achieve a successful and productive retirement. If success, for you, has to be accompanied by profit, then concentrate on your fastball only. That's where you will do your best work. Many retirees measure success in their retirement life by the satisfaction they get in doing things for others. There are so many ways you can use those God-given talents that don't fall into the "fastball" category, we don't want you to discard them. Let's save these for future reference.

Don't Procrastinate

Right now you probably think the Franklin/Hauser stock-taking system isn't so bad. You're probably saying to yourself: "It'll take some time, but I can do it . . . as soon as I can get around to it."

You can come up with all kinds of excuses for not getting started right away, but what could be more important to you right now? This is the beginning of the rest of your life. Is anything more important to you than having a successful and productive retirement? This is not work! It's your future we're talking about. You might have used some of the same excuses for other things you've put off. Keep in mind the objective is to get you out of that rocking chair, out from in front of the TV set, and out doing something you want to do and enjoy!

I'll level with you. If you've followed through on this exercise, you've found your fastball. But honestly, I can't force you to follow through. You're an adult, and you're going to have to decide what's best for you. You're the only one who can do it. You're the only one who can make the best decision about what you want to do for the rest of your life.

It's Not All Chin to the Wind

I won't kid you about it. Most successful retirees I've known, read about, and studied have gone through a period of turmoil, either before or after they retired. I know a number of early retirees who would rather be working on the job they once had, but that job is no longer there. It disappeared in an organizational reshuffle, or the company reduced its work force and offered attractive retirement packages to those who retired early.

Some of these people never got around to working on Step Number One until most of their options for doing it the easy way had evaporated. Some were financially broken before they realized the pension they were receiving would not support them the rest of their lives. Some had retired with enough money to keep them for the rest of their lives but then made poor investments and saw their funds dwindle away. Others had plenty of money but longed for the self-respect and prestige they had before.

"Dear God," they pleaded, "isn't there one thing in me that matters? Isn't there one thing left in me that I can build on? I just want some dignity and productivity in my life. I still have a lot to offer, in spite of my age. Isn't there one thing left that somebody can use and that will give me a feeling of self-worth?"

Then they went out and took their inventory. They found one or two true talents, and they used them to put their lives back together—better than before.

By now, some of you have taken your personal inventory, or tried to take it, as we asked you to do earlier in this chapter. Knowing human nature, though, we know some of you will read right to the end of this chapter before you start. There's not much time for procrastination now. We just want to remind you there are some things we do well and with ease. Those are the things we can't remember not being able to do well. And no matter which category you fall into, you should take another look at your personal inventory now. You might want to add to or revise the list.

Talents aren't necessarily big Edison- or Kissinger-sized things. An even temper, a skill at taking grief from people, or just a sunny disposition are all talents. So are high energy, little need for sleep, and seeing work as fun. You have to realize that no matter how meager or simple your talents may appear, they can work wonders for you if you want them to.

So make it a priority to set aside whatever time is required to take your own personal inventory. You can use the pages that follow, or you can use a plain sheet of paper if your list is too long. Give this project all the time and energy it deserves. When you have completed your inventory, we have another short exercise to help you get to know yourself.

Rules for Effective Personal Inventory Taking

1. Make it a TOP priority. This is extremely important for you and your future. Right now, you're the most important person in your world.

2. Pick a date and vow nothing will interfere with it. This date is as important as a meeting with your lawyer or minister on crucial or serious business or personal matters.

3. Plan on a minimum of two continuous hours to complete your inventory.

4. Pick a quiet place away from people, telephones, TV, or any other possible interruptions.

5. Be rested and fresh. If possible, write your inventory the first thing in the morning, when your mind is clearest and has the fewest external pressures.

6. Have plenty of paper, pens, or pencils and whatever else you may need to do the whole job at one sitting.

Congratulations and Good Luck!

WORKSHEET NUMBER 1.

Step One

Get to Know Yourself

My Fastballs

Strengths, talents, and things I like to do.

STEP ONE

WORKSHEET NUMBER 2.

Step One

Get to Know Yourself

My Change-ups

**Weaknesses: Things I'm not
very good at and don't like to do.**

27

WORKSHEET NUMBER 3.

**Additional thoughts
and insights on my strengths
and things I like to do.**

S<u>TEP</u> T<u>WO</u>

TRANSITION TO RETIREMENT ACTIVITY

The number of options open to you in your retirement can be mind boggling. We don't think anyone wants to sit in the old rocker and be useless— useless to themselves and to humanity—but you must keep active or it will happen to you.

You've found your fastball now, but you need a game to play in and a chance to show your stuff. Maybe you're still a little puzzled about how or when to use the fastball, even though you know you want to use it 80 to 90 percent of the time. There are people out there who want to use your talents. Some will want it for free, and you might want to give it to them for free. That's up to you. But first, let's take a look at the transition process.

You Have Alternatives

You might decide your fastball is just exactly what you were doing when you worked on your regular job.

But now the situation has changed. You have choices. You have years of experience. You don't have to be tied down working for just one employer. You can work whatever hours you want. You can be a consultant!

What is a consultant? Clarify your own expectations of what a consultant in your field of work actually does. You can do this by talking with someone in that field who is actually working as a consultant.

You'll find a consultant doesn't just do the same work you once did. A consultant must maintain an office, write proposals, distinguish between the initial problem and the underlying problems. A consultant must know how to ask questions. A consultant must be able to write reports and present them orally. So, if you think your fastball is going to lead you into consulting, go into it with your eyes wide open.

What about other alternatives? That's where you might have to spend time doing some creative thinking. I know a retired Episcopal priest who's happy as a bump on a log, serving as a director of a Y-Uncles' program. I never did ask him if he is getting paid for the job. It doesn't really matter. He's busy every day with the work he has chosen. He recruits and checks out the character of the men who will serve as "uncles" for fatherless boys. He tries to match them up with their "nephews" by locality, personality, etc. He trains the new "uncles", and he plans things for them to do individually and collectively. This retired priest's fastball was working with people. He is still doing it and is every bit as effective as he was before retirement.

Let's take a look at some of the things other people have done before retirement and what they decided to do after retirement. It might give you some ideas.

I know a man who was an FBI agent. When he retired from the FBI, he decided to run for district judge. He won and served in that office for many years. Now, he's retired from the judgeship but is called to fill in occasionally.

I know a man who was a corporate pilot. He's retired now but has been a valuable assistant to the local airport board in managing their airfields and searching for a new commuter airline to service the city. He also has been asked to serve as a consultant to a small local industry that has only one plane, but that industry has recently been purchased by an international conglomerate. He might end up being an international consultant without even trying!

That's what we mean when we talk about a *transition* to retirement activity. It's that simple idea of using your best pitch 80 to 90 percent of the time. It's being able to step back and look at yourself and see what you're doing while you're right in the middle of doing it. It's matching your talents with the right opportunity—at the right time.

Colonel Sanders is our number one example of a person who made a great transition and turned what he did best into more than a million dollars in a few short years. Here are some examples of the "before" and "after" for other retirees. Maybe something will spark your interest.

Before Retirement Jobs and Hobbies	*After Retirement Jobs and Activities*
Priest/Preacher	Director of Y-Uncles
FBI Agent	Judge
Business communicator (and many others)	Author/Writer Free-lance writer
Policeman	Store detective, Security guard
Art director or layout manager	Portrait artist or landscape artist

•*If you're an office professional or manager* . . . . . Manage your church office, etc.

•*If you're a good cook.* . . . . Give cooking lessons, sell what you make best, write a cookbook, demonstrate food, or work at the local food kitchen

•*High level manager or Corporate Officer (and don't need the money).* . . . . Member of library board or other civic board . . . . Involvement in fund drives

•*If you like to meet people.* . . . . .Consider party planning, bartending, running for public office, working for your political party, or being host or hostess at a restaurant or working at a fast-food establishment

•*If your hobby is woodworking.* . . . . . .Furniture repair or refinishing, etc.

•*If you're good at gardening.* . . . . Turn it into a business

•*If you like to read* . . . . .Help others learn to read or volunteer at your library

•*If sales is your fastball.* . . . . You can always find something to sell

•*Accountant* . . . . Part-time book-keeper for small business or charity.

This list could go on and on. Did it start you thinking about some of the things you might do in retirement? Did you notice that most of the after retirement activities were very different from the before retirement jobs? That's what we're trying to get across to you. Your opportunities are unlimited. Your fastball might be in your hobby and not at all related to the job you worked at most of your life. Your local library is an excellent resource for information if you want more ideas.

Income Isn't Always Top Priority

This list includes activities that will keep you busy, keep you involved, or maintain your prestige. They might not add to your income. We could add many other activities, such as Meals on Wheels or volunteering at a hospital, church, or civic organization.

The point is it's not always necessary to work at an income-producing job after retirement. In fact, getting paid can be demeaning for some people. The important goal should be to keep busy, because that contributes greatly to good health. So, look around and see what there is for you to do.

Maybe You're a Writer

Let's take a look at another item on the "before" and "after" list. We mentioned that business communicators and many others could logically be authors or free-lance writers. Have you ever given any thought to being a writer? There are so many things to write about. Some will produce profit; some won't.

Take, for example, a fellow I know who was involved with plant safety. Shortly before he retired, he decided to write one of those little 12-page safety pamphlets similar to one he had been using all his working life. He submitted his work to a company whose name was listed on the back of one of the pamphlets he had been distributing. Imagine his surprise when his work was accepted. And there was an even greater surprise when he received his first royalty check. General Motors had ordered thousands of the pamphlets and other companies followed suit. He showed me a royalty check for $5,000. He continued writing these pamphlets after retirement.

Does this little anecdote strike a spark? Maybe you can reach into your bag of tools and come up with something just as saleable. You don't have to be a Hemingway. You don't have to write the world's greatest novel. You have a lifetime of experience, and someone might be interested in something you know.

On the other hand, I have a friend who has a heart problem. He retired a little early, after heart surgery. He did a little consulting work, but it was just too strenuous, and he had enough money to lead a comfortable life. The heart has grown weaker, but my friend's interests keep him going. He's an author, too, but he's not trying to sell his work. He's writing a history of his family. The research is incredible, including some extended trips to areas where some of his distant relatives live. Because of his heart condition, he can't do much physical work, and he might not live to be 92 years old like the Colonel. But he's living a full, enjoyable life and his mind is as sharp as a tack.

There's one thing about writing. It can be as inexpensive, or as expensive, as you want to make it. You can use a pencil, an old beaten up typewriter, or you can invest in a computer and word processing equipment. It might be difficult for you to convince a publisher to use your work if it's hand written. So if you're serious about writing, you might consider learning to use a typewriter or computer. That's a challenge in itself.

We haven't mentioned cost yet, but you're going to have expenses no matter what business venture you decide on. If it's a computer for writing, you'll have to figure the cost of the computer, the computer program, the paper, the postage, and anything else you might "need", including office furniture. Of course, they say the only difference between men and boys is in the cost of their toys. Well! I have to admit that I bought my first computer shortly before I retired and have now up-graded to a larger one. My only excuse was I knew I was going to have to write a lot of letters, and my handwriting was terrible. Whatever your reason, if you want to look at your retirement life realistically, you'll have to face up to the expenses, especially first-year expenses.

It's time now for another short work session. But before you write anything, look at the sample work sheets on the next two pages. These show how the start-up needs of two people can differ greatly for essentially the same post-retirement activity. Incidentally, the pre-retirement job classifications have no meaning in these examples.

You should "cost-out" several of your top selections, even though you have, at this moment, decided what your fastball is and you're going with it.

It's going to take some figuring and maybe some research to list what you'll need in the way of equipment to start some businesses and to figure the cost for equipment. You might need a calculator and some catalogs in addition to extra paper for working out your own cost estimate. The examples on the next pages should stimulate your thought process so you can be more factual as you compile your own cost estimate.

Once you've studied the two sample pages you should have a better idea of how to proceed with your own cost estimate. Don't bypass this exercise, and take enough time here to thoroughly analyze your situation.

If you're planning to go into any kind of business, you might want to talk to friends who have gone through the same experience. You might seek professional advice to help you decide whether you want to incorporate the business. You can operate a small business without incorporating.

Don't delay your work on your own cost estimate chart any longer than is necessary to get the information you need to enter on the chart. In fact, your best plan of attack would be to start filling in the columns on the next page right now, as soon as you finish reading this page. Use the facts you have at hand, including cost estimates. You can make changes as you get specific details about costs and as you decide whether you want to incorporate or not.

Most people can't tell an opportunity from an avocado. They're not trained to look objectively at the rich array of alternatives facing them. But that's what we're asking you to do here. That's why we asked you to look at more than one job or activity. Good luck! You'll be surprised how easy your decision will be after you fill out this chart.

Sample Worksheet—Retirement Activity

A High-Cost Deluxe Estimate

Before Retirement Jobs and Hobbies	After Retirement Jobs and Activities	Cost Estimate for First Year of the Activity	
Personnel Manager	Author/Writer	New computer	$1249.00
		Color Monitor	$449.00
		Hard Drive for computer	$400.00
		Software for computer	$500.00
		Printer for computer	$400.00
		Computer/printer supplies	$100.00
		Printed letterhead	$70.00
		Paper and office supplies	$100.00
		Postage	$100.00
		Used copy machine	$500.00
		Re-do room for office	$500.00
		Incorporate as a business	$200.00
		Business telephone	$300.00
			$4868.00

Sample Worksheet—Retirement Activity

Low-Cost Estimate

Before Retirement Jobs and Hobbies	After Retirement Jobs and Activities	Cost Estimate for First Year of the Activity	
Shop Foreman	Author/Writer	Use typewriter I own	$ 00.00
		Use desk in my study	$ 00.00
		Use of copy machine	$ 25.00
		Paper and office supplies	$ 25.00
		Postage	$ 10.00
			$ 60.00

Worksheet

Your Own Retirement Activity

Before Retirement Jobs and Hobbies	After Retirement Jobs and Activities

Your Own Cost Estimate

First Year of Activity

There you are! You've done it! If you've filled out your own cost estimate on the previous page, you've taken a big step toward that active and profitable retirement.

There are so many trite old sayings designed to set our lives in order that we sometimes don't know which ones to follow. For example, you'd be a little confused if you tried to heed all the advice given in the sayings that follow: "Don't look a gift horse in the mouth." "Opportunity knocks but once." "Strike while the iron is hot." "He who hesitates is lost." Most likely you wouldn't be reading this book and working through these exercises. You'd probably be jumping at every opportunity that comes along, instead of finding your fastball and deciding what's out there for you.

Many people, when they retire, find themselves with an indefinite future. They head for home and hunker in for the rest of their lives, afraid to move. I guess we're all old enough to remember Mae West. One of her favorite sayings was: "Life is a banquet and most people are starving to death." She was right. Lots of retirees behave as if they are starving to death. They won't spend a nickel for their own pleasure, or for the improvement of their lifestyle and personal satisfaction. Thoreau once said, "The mass of people live out their lives in quiet desperation." If Thoreau were living now, he could have added, "And when they die, their children buy new homes and automobiles."

A Harvard Professor by the name of Dr. Harry Levinson estimates that 80 percent of all working people are unsuited for the jobs they hold. Maybe that was true for you before you retired. Maybe the sharp edges of your ambition were beaten into dull plowshares.

But this retirement thing is an entirely new ballgame. Here's your chance to do what's best for you, or to put it another way: Here's your chance to do what you do best. Now that you have a solid awareness of your own abilities, you should have the courage to move from a situation that might have been discouraging and maybe even a little frightening into "the rest of your life." Your plan should be taking shape now. The door is ready to open on a productive and happy future.

Were You One of These?

John Haney is a good friend of mine and an officer in a large bank. John was talking about his bank employees one day when he said they have two types of people who quit. There are those who quit and leave and those who quit and stay on the payroll. He said the ones who quit and stay are desperately unhappy with their jobs and challenges. Unfortunately this group doesn't have the guts to leave the job, even though they are so miserable. They refuse to believe it's their resistance to change that's at the root of their problems. *You* might have been one of those unhappy workers. Now's the time to make a *right* choice.

For Some, Work is Fun

I have often wondered if the reason there are so many recreation vehicles is that people want to get as far away from their daily grind as possible. A group of industrial psychologists asked several hundred people to make believe they'd suddenly won a million dollars. The psychologists then asked the following question: "Would you continue to work?" More than 75 percent said: "Heck, yes. Who wants to hang around home all day doing nothing?"

I went with my wife to the local supermarket. The bag boy was just a bit older than I am. He's about 75. He told me he loves the work. He got tired of sitting home watching the "boob tube." Maybe you saw the 83-year-old man on Johnny Carson's program recently. He's been bagging groceries for ten years. He said the regular customers at the supermarket wait in line to have him bag their groceries, even when they could go through the express line. The man told Johnny he has no plans to retire from this job because he loves it.

That's what it's all about: doing something you do well and feeling good about. In other words, you should be looking for something to do where you can throw your fastball 80 to 90 percent of the time. One of my favorite quotes is from John D. Rockefeller. "If your goal is to become rich," he said, "you will never achieve it."

I agree with John D. Your goal should be to match your talents to the right opportunity, whether it's a job, vocation, or mission in life. What better time is there than right now, when your life is in a state of flux, to be very selective about what you're going to do for the rest of your life. Your choice of what you're going to do in retirement should turn you on so much you can't wait to get at it. That's the way it should be, and that's the way it will be, when you've mastered the process we outline for you here.

Search for the Right Opportunities

So, how do you find the right opportunity? After all, about 5,800 Americans become 65 years old every day, and some retire long before age 65. One thing you should not be doing is going around asking friends and relatives for advice. Relatives and well-meaning friends will love to give you advice about what you should be doing, but they're usually just taking their own pulses. The advice you'll get from them is what they wish they would have done, could have done, or had the nerve to do with their own lives.

Ask for their advice and you'll hear something like this. "You know, I often look back and wish I would have become a professional porcupine plucker when I retired. That field is really booming. It doesn't cost much to buy into it. There's lots of room for growth in that porcupine plucking business, and no one has a franchise in this town. I can tell you'd be good at it, and you know prorcupine pluckers make good money."

It doesn't matter what field they're pushing. No matter what it is, it's got to be your field to be good—to be right for you. They haven't identified your fastball. They don't know your innermost desires and needs. You can't wear another person's boots, and they can't wear yours. You've got to be comfortable, and you've got to do your own thing.

In the last chapter you identified and evaluated your talents and skills. You found the special few that will help to make your retirement a success. Already in this chapter, you have taken those special few talents and skills that you feel most comfortable with and you've put together a cost estimate for the first year of activity. Now comes the matching of those goals with the opportunities out there.

Don't rush. Don't worry about what you've done to date. You need to look around. If you're like a lot of retirees, you've worked for the same company for a number of years and haven't had the experience of looking for a new job for many years. So where do you start now? Remember, you know what you want to do. Stick to your goal. You might even turn down some jobs or activities offered to you because they are not what you want to do. What the heck! You have retirement income. You'll wait until the time is right.

Now, here's why I want you to stick to your goal and turn down any job or activity that isn't what you want to do. I have just read an article in a recent issue of *Modern Maturity*, the magazine of the American Association of Retired Persons. The story was about a butcher named John who was meat manager for a chain of supermarkets in Pennsylvania. He tried several times to retire and go into some other field, but his boss always wanted him to stay.

Finally John did retire, but he agreed to work in one of the stores on a schedule of his choosing, which turned out to be 20 to 30 hours each week. He still dreams of a second career reporting on hotel accommodations, but he's too involved with the meat department to make that dream come true. He even spent his last vacation checking the meat departments of other supermarkets for pointers to bring back to his employer. Wouldn't you say John needs to do what you've just been doing? Find his fastball and then aim for the target.

At this point a story about my father, Lee Hauser, comes to mind. As I mentioned earlier, my father had always been a great help to me in my quest for success. He ended up doing more for me than I ever imagined.

To help celebrate my 35th birthday, he and my mother drove out from St. Paul to our home in Greenwich,

Connecticut. It was a joyous period for all of us. They were pleased and proud of my progress, and I was delighted to share some of my success first hand, including our growing family and my Wall Street activities.

One evening, my dad and I were having a warm, relaxed chat in the library when he shared a dream with me. He proceeded to tell me his secret goal for years had been to go into business for himself when he retired. He went on to say in just two years he would have earned maximum retirement benefits from his job with the U.S. Government. Then he'd be free to start his own full-time business making wooden toys in his basement.

He'd been making toys for years as a hobby, and so he could make some extra money to help put my brother and me through school. He bubbled with excitement as he described the way he would set up the shop and distribute the finished products.

I was delighted and pleased to see my dad, who had worked 42 years for the same government agency, now on the verge of achieving his goal in life. Now, in two years, he would be ready, willing, and able to become an entrepreneur and start his own business. It was quite an evening for both of us.

My mom and dad left a few days later, and our lives returned to normal. But, a few months after they got home and before my dad could retire, my brother called with the chilling news that dad had died suddenly from a massive heart attack.

All during our trip back to St. Paul and through the funeral arrangements and burial service, that conversation with dad in my library kept running through my head. He had taken the ball in his own end zone and by hard work, determination, and dedication had carried it all the way down the field to the five-yard line. He was ready to score a touchdown—ready to retire and launch a new career that had been his burning ambition for the last twenty years of his life. He was ready to become an entrepreneur and be in business for himself, making the most of his God-given talents and being deliriously happy doing it. But the game ended before he could make his dream come true.

I'm not in medical science, and I don't pretend to be clairvoyant, but I have a very strong feeling that if my dad had settled for early retirement to pursue his toy-making dreams and had stopped going down to the post office on Kellogg Boulevard several years earlier, he would have added twenty years to his life. He also would have added loads of satisfaction to himself, my mother, our whole family, and certainly to his customers. He might have even become the Colonel Sanders of the toy industry.

As sad as that event was for me, Dad had once again given me a piece of invaluable advice. If you want to do something so badly that it becomes a persistent voice in your conscious and subconscious thoughts, then DO IT! Believe me. It will be much better for you and everyone around you.

At this point, you can be compared with a kernel of popcorn. You won't reach your potential unless you're heated up. Once the heat is applied, you can see and feel the change taking place until you reach the point where you will pop open into something white and fluffy, much larger than you were in the kernel. But not all the kernels "pop". Some pop out of the pan before they're totally heated up and some get lost among the popped kernels and don't reach the popping temperature. Some of the kernels pop and expand for a while to their full potential but then lie in the bottom of the pan too long. They get burned and become useless.

I'm sure you can see the moral of this little parable. If you have that burning desire to go into business for yourself, go for it! If you have found your fastball, if your figures in the last worksheet showed you could swing it physically and financially, *now* is the time to do it. Such a decision is never going to be any easier. There will be no right time. There will always be reasons for keeping your dreams on "hold."

When is the Right Time?

I'll never forget the piece of advice I got from Ronnie Brukenfeld, a friend and fellow member of the New York Stock Exchange. I met Ronnie when I was a young lad, just beginning to trade on the floor of the Exchange. He was many years my senior in age, experience, and wisdom, but he befriended me and became my mentor.

One day I learned he had established his firm in 1932, in the middle of the Great Depression. I was amazed and curious to know how in the world he could have decided to start trading stock at such a historically lousy time. From everything I'd read, Wall Street in 1932 was pretty grim. You had to keep looking up as you walked down the street to avoid being hit by a bankrupt broker who'd thrown himself out of a sky-scraper window.

I'll never forget Ronnie's response to my question of how and when he got started. He stopped short, moved in real close, looked over his bifocals at me, and addressed me in a slow deliberate voice. "Leo," he said, "if you want to do something badly enough, it's always the right time." For Ronnie, with his burning desire and deep commitment, 1932 was the right time to go into business.

Naturally we don't know what direction you're headed or what decision you made about your post-retirement job or activities, because you are the one who made the choice. Since one choice could be going into business for yourself, we'd better cover that in a little more detail.

Many people go into business for the wrong reasons. They say, "I'm tired of being bossed around. I've listened to bosses all my working life. Now that I'm retired, it's my turn. The owners have all the fun and money, so why not me? Can those attitudes have anything to do with the fact that 85 percent of all new businesses fail within the first two years?

Many of the country's most successful businesses would never have gotten started if their founders had the slightest idea how much work it was going to be. Still, it's an attractive option, and it's one that you have a perfect right to consider and accept or reject. Just keep in mind that the success you achieve in the business will depend to a great degree on how much "blood, sweat, and tears" you put into the project.

Fundamentals of Business Success

Here are some things I know about running a business. I learned them from my own experience and from observing other successful people.

Thomas Edison said, "Invention is two percent inspiration and 98 percent perspiration." That's true of success in any endeavor, especially in starting your own business. Success starts after 5 p.m. and continues through the weekends. The difference between a job and a career is about twenty hours a week. Sometimes, you even get to work on holidays.

Successful people invest in themselves. They go to seminars, they read a lot, and they consult with others. They're natural and eager learners. You don't necessarily have to go back to school if you're starting a new business, but you do have to learn everything there is to know about it. You need to learn from every encounter you have with people in the business, and you have to make sure there are lots of encounters if you're new in the business.

Successful people do not get involved with get-rich-quick schemes. Whether it's a lottery ticket, a tip on a long-shot, or a match-book cover come-on, you can bet really successful people will turn their backs on it. The reason is simple. Successful people believe they're in control of their lives and fates. They know effort means more than luck. They know that praying isn't a substitute for planning and that pie-in-the-sky is just dodo-bird food.

Now, don't misunderstand me. You'll frequently hear me say, "Let go and let God." I believe that because so

29427

many things have happened to me that I didn't plan for and couldn't have planned for. I accept the fact there is spontaneity in life—an element of the unknown and a power behind me. But I also know that no one ever succeeded by staying in bed all day, waiting for their ship to come in.

A key point in one of my favorite inspirational books, *Jonathan Livingston Seagull*, is "He who flies highest sees farthest." A surprising number of golden opportunities seem to open up for those people who work hardest at putting themselves on the success path and who look for opportunities. For these people, the unexpected always seems to happen. But in a way, that's not true. Those people who work hardest at putting themselves on the path to success have a real desire to accomplish something. They have the guts to be themselves. They make their opportunities. Good luck is a loser's estimate of a winner's success.

Successful people help others succeed. The Bible says, "Cast bread upon the waters." Now, it doesn't say, "Try it once, and if it works, good. If not . . ." No, it just says "cast", and like fly fishing, you have to keep on casting in order to catch anything worth keeping.

The same goes for people. Successful people extend themselves to others, but not with the thought of immediate return. They know if they extend themselves to others, help will be given back to them sometime in the future.

Successful people are not jealous or resentful of other people's success. Successful people are encouraged, not discouraged, by the good things that happen to people around them. It is a waste of time to be angry and resentful about the success of people around you. Successful people cannot afford to waste time like that. My favorite religious hymn is "Let there be peace on earth and let it begin with me." I really feel that way. There aren't enough hours in my life to waste one split second resenting another person's success.

Successful people have supreme self-confidence. They believe their ideas are as good, if not better, than anyone else's. They feel if they are given an even break, they will win the medal, gain the gold, and overcome every obstacle.

Successful people believe the best investment they can make is an investment in themselves. After all, they're the best and brightest people they know. If they're going to gamble on an investment, they're going to make sure it's an investment in themselves.

That's how I feel about success in general and what I know about successful people, entrepreneurs in particular, that I have known.

Although we've been talking about the *"Fundamentals of Business Success"* there's not one thing we've said that cannot be applied to success in a job working for someone else. Owning your own business isn't for everyone—especially owning a retirement business. If the risk of owning your own business seems too great or if you just don't want to be bothered with your own business at this time in life, don't despair. There's nothing degrading about working for someone else, whether it be on a full-time job, a part-time job, or a volunteer job. So let's assume you are going to be looking for a new retirement job, one that fits all the needs you've already listed.

Looking for Job Opportunities

Regardless of whether you've decided to strike out on your own and form a new company, keep on doing the same types of work you've always done, try to turn a hobby into a paying business, or contribute your time to community projects, success is never accomplished on automatic pilot. You're going to have to do things differently than you did before, as well as doing some things you've never done before.

Success comes from using your talents the best way you can. Before you were retired, your talents and achievements were well known within your corporation and by your friends and colleagues. Now, even if you plan to seek the same type of employment, probably on a part-time basis, you will most likely be dealing with different people in a different company. Your need to show proof of expertise will be even greater if you have decided that one of your hobbies is really your fastball.

You have to stand on the pitchers mound and throw the strikes. No one can do it for you. You do, however, need support. Every pitcher needs a catcher and a team to work with. Your success will be supported, nurtured, and aided by many people who you must reach out to help, just as surely as they must reach out and help you. If you're looking for a job, you need "team" support.

Who's on the team at this time? Let's field a team with your old bosses at the catcher's position, co-workers at first base, friends at second base, relatives at third, and union, club, and professional associates in the field. Don't forget the members of your church or synagogue are also members of the team.

It pays to advertise, and the more contact you have with members of your team, the more you let them know what you want, the more likely you are to get it. That's it! Let the whole team know. They're your team. They'll probably have some leads as to where you can find exactly the retirement job you want. Or if you're starting your own business, they can steer customers your way.

If you're looking for a full- or part-time retirement job, make a list of the local employers known to hire people in the line of work you want to get into. Don't overlook any of the hiring services. They will be listed in your telephone book under Employment Agencies or Employment Contractors–Temporary.

Some of the temporary employment agencies have contracts with local employers to help the retired employee back into the company on part-time or full-time jobs. In most of these arrangements, the employment agency becomes the employer and pays the salary and benefits. Many of the management and technical recruiting organizations also have job openings that are suitable for retirees.

There are a lot more things you can do to search out a retirement job. I told you earlier that your local library is an excellent source of information when you're looking for retirement activities. Now, as you're looking for employment in your retirement years, the library is again an excellent resource. There you can find trade papers and magazines you might not have access to in any other way. These usually carry "help

RETIREMENT: NEW BEGINNINGS, NEW CHALLENGES

wanted" advertising. If not, there will be articles about companies and advertising from companies you might want to contact. The local papers are at the library too, and the library is a good place to get off by yourself to think about some of the possibilities open to you in your retirement.

Before we leave this chapter, we have one more worksheet for your planning. We just want to help you organize your thoughts and put down on paper just who you plan to contact for help. Specifically, what companies or organizations do you want to contact about jobs, volunteer positions, or help in the new business you're planning? There's a place for you to put a date to do these thing, too. Enter the date, and let's see how close you can stick to the schedule.

Good luck! You should spend at least a half hour completing this chart. An hour would be better. It will take longer if you go to the library to do some research.

Planning My Contacts

My retirement activity will be:

_____

Name_____

Address_____

Phone_____

Date _____

Name _____

Address _____

Phone_____

Date_____

Name _____

Address_____

Phone_____

Date _____

Don't stop here.
Your list could include 10 to 15 people.

Name_____

Address_____

Phone_____

Date_____

Name_____

Address_____

Phone_____

Date_____

Name_____

Address_____

Phone_____

Date_____

Name_____

Address_____

Phone_____

Date_____

I will contact these businesses

Company _____

Contact Person _____

Address _____

Phone _____

Date _____

Company _____

Contact Person _____

Address _____

Phone _____

Date _____

If you want to do something badly enough . . . it's always the right time.

Company _____

Contact Person _____

Address _____

Phone _____

Date _____

Company _____

Contact Person _____

Address _____

Phone _____

Date _____

Company _____

Contact Person _____

Address _____

Phone _____

Date _____

STEP THREE

SET BIG GOALS FOR THE REST OF YOUR LIFE

This chapter will help you decide where you want to go and what you want to accomplish in your retirement life. The essence of goal setting is captured in this old German proverb. "You have to take life as it happens, but you should try to make it happen the way you want to take it."

Here's a poem that comes to mind, too. It was written by Ella Wheeler Wilcox. It's particularly appropriate as you make your decision about what you are going to do for "the rest of your life."

61

The Winds of Fate

One ship drives east and another drives west
With the selfsame winds that blow
'Tis the set of the sails
And not the gales
Which tell us the way to go.

Like the winds of the sea are the ways of fate
As we voyage along through life
'Tis the set of a soul
That decides its goal
And not the calm or the strife.

Now there's some good and helpful advice to cling to as you chart your course for the "rest of your life."

As I've told you before, I'm fond of saying, "Let go and let God." It captures my belief that you can't plan for some of the best things that will happen to you in this life. But, I believe just as emphatically in the words of career development psychologist David P. Campbell. "If you don't know where you're going," said Mr. Campbell, "you'll probably end up somewhere else."

You have to choose the direction you want the rest of your life to take. You have to set goals and be prepared to be surprised as well. Let me be very clear about the paradox involved in setting goals on one hand and staying open to opportunity and surprise on the other.

I believe life is a journey—not a destination. I believe joy is as much in the running as in the arriving. The key is to move in a positive fashion in the direction of your hopes and dreams, through goals that are both practical and powerful. So when I'm talking about setting goals, I'm talking about great big, exciting goals. I'm talking about the goals for "the rest of your life."

How big should goals be? As big as Michelangelo included in his prayers. "Lord," he prayed, "grant that I may always desire more than I can accomplish." Wouldn't it be great if every retiree woke up every morning with that prayer on his or her lips and a bright outlook on life. Big, far reaching goals have a way of pulling the best from us; of getting us started in the morning; of giving us the incentive to work harder to focus on success and to maximize our efforts.

How big should your goals be? We're talking about the kind of goals that a school teacher in Milwaukee, Wisconsin, had. Her dream was simply to be a part of establishing a country where people of her religious conviction could worship with dignity and freedom. She met her goal and then some.

Do you know who that was? Golda Meir. Here was a woman, born in Russia, raised and educated in the United States, who was destined to be one of the most powerful women in the world. Even when she was a grandmother, she was Prime Minister of Israel and one of the great statespersons of her time.

How Big is Big?

How big is a big goal? Golda's goal was so big it stayed with her all of her life—beginning when she was five years old and was almost killed on the streets of Pinsk by Cossack horsemen.

It depends on where you are when you dream your dream and set your goal as to how big is big. For a millionaire, making another hundred thousand dollars is not a big thing, but for a little Chicano lady with a four-foot by four-foot taco stand, it's a whale of a wish. If you don't already know the story of Ramona Banuelos, now is a good time to tell you about her.

You say you've never heard of her? Well, I'm sure you have, but let me tell the story anyway. Ramona Banuelos was 16 years old and living in Mexico when she got married. Two years and two sons later, she was divorced and left to raise her family by herself. She was determined to provide a life of dignity and pride for herself and her two sons.

After crossing the Rio Grande into the United States with all her worldly possessions knotted up in a simple shawl, she ended up in El Paso, Texas. There she worked in a laundry for a dollar a day. But she never lost her commitment to build a respectable life in the shadow of poverty.

While she was working in Texas, she heard there were more opportunities in California. So, with seven dollars in her pocket, she and her two sons boarded a bus to Los Angeles. She started out washing dishes and taking jobs where she could find them.

She saved as much money as she could. When she had four hundred dollars, she and her aunt bought a little tortilla shop that had one tortilla-making machine and one grinder. They were so successful making tortillas that they were soon able to open other shops. When the aunt found the work to be too hard, young Ramona bought her share of the business.

The years flew by and before long, the little tortilla shops grew to become Ramona's Mexican Food Products, the largest Mexican wholesale food concern in the nation at that time, employing more than 300 people.

Having achieved financial security for herself and her sons, this brave young woman turned her energies to improving the standard of living for her fellow Mexican-Americans.

"We need our own bank," she thought, and before long, she and a handful of friends had founded the Pan-American National Bank in East Los Angeles. The bank was dedicated to serving the Mexican-American community. Today, the bank's resources have grown to more than 22 million dollars, with 86 percent of the depositors being of Latin-American ancestry.

This woman's success in banking didn't come easily. The negative-thinking experts told her she couldn't do it. "Mexican-Americans can't start their own bank," they said. "You are not qualified to start a bank. You'll never make it." She quietly said, "I can, and I will."

She and her partners opened their bank in a little trailer. Selling stock to the community posed another problem, since the Mexican-American people she was trying to help didn't have faith in themselves. When she asked them to buy stock in the new bank, they declined. "What makes you think we can have a bank?" they asked. "We've tried before and failed. Don't you see, Mexican people are not bankers?" But she persevered, and today that bank is one of the great success stories of East Los Angeles.

Do you still think you've never heard of Ramona Banuelos? If you're observant, you've seen her name hundreds of times and even carried it around in your pocket, billfold, or purse. Ramona Banuelos moved on to even higher achievements after the Pan-American Bank success. She became the thirty-fourth Treasurer of the United States, and her signature appeared on millions of dollars of U.S. currency.

Can you imagine that? A little Mexican immigrant who had a big dream and went on to become the treasurer of the largest financial entity in the world? Ramona Banuelos, with all those fantastic credits to her name, is now back in California. You can bet she's dreaming new dreams and setting new goals. And she's doing it with that special knowledge that a goal is simply a dream with a deadline.

It's those big goals that make you pop out of bed in the morning and look for the new experience—the project that you want to complete that day or that week. And once you've reached the peak, there's always something beyond if we keep updating our goals. This should apply to you in retirement, just as it should have applied to you during your work life.

So, how big is big? I'll give you a simple test of your goals. If your best friends don't laugh at you when you tell them your goal, it isn't big enough. That's true. It happened to me quite often. In fact, it happened to me as I was telling a friend, who is retired, about the purpose of this book and the fact I was writing this chapter on goals—BIG GOALS. "I don't need goals now that I'm retired," he said. "I'm busy all the time. I get up at the same time every day. I work in the yard. I play golf. Who needs goals when they're retired?"

I could have replied, "What you've just told me demonstrates that you need some goals." It's evident to me his life could be a lot more interesting and exciting if he had some goals that involved him with community affairs or with helping other people. Routine can lead to monotony. Monotony can lead to boredom. Boredom can lead to excessive drinking and smoking. Excessive drinking and smoking—or just sitting in a rocking chair—can lead to poor health. And one of our goals is to keep you happy, healthy, and to give you a long life.

Personal Satisfaction is Important

Big goals don't necessarily have a dollar sign attached to them. Not every retiree wants or needs to earn more money. It's great if there's some income attached to your goal! But there are plenty of big goals that don't have income as a payoff and do provide a lot of personal satisfaction. Here are some examples:

Complete or continue your formal education.

Travel extensively. Take a trip around the world.

Join the Peace Corps.

Write a book.

Take on a volunteer assignment at your local library, hospital, school system, soup kitchen, etc.

*Enter politics, either as a
candidate for office or as
a volunteer worker for your party.*

If, on the other hand, your goals do include an income-producing project, here's a challenge for you. If your banker doesn't turn green, or worse yet, if he likes your idea and agrees with your goal, then you're not shooting high enough. It's a good indication that your goal is not imaginative enough or grand enough to keep you excited and motivated for very long.

If you banker looks at you as if his backbone has turned to wrought iron or if your mother-in-law whispers to your spouse, "See, dear. I told you this would happen," then and only then is your goal big enough.

Shoot for the Moon

Our country was founded on big dreams. Our founding fathers and mothers set big goals and dreamed of things people of their time couldn't even imagine. We're still a young country, not much more than 200 years old, but as I stand at attention reciting the Pledge of Allegiance at my civic club meetings and sing the National Anthem, I know we live in a country where we can become what we want to be, even after we retire. We can be as successful, happy, sad, mediocre, enslaved, or free as we care to be—as long as we work at it. I know I can shoot for the moon because that's what America is all about. And if I miss a little, I'll still land up among the stars.

Now, why is it important for us to have goals and objectives when we are retired? What's the alternative? You can sit in front of the TV and watch the CNN news all day now. You can hear the news over and over. It's just a repeat of the six o'clock news that tells us everything bad that is happening around the world. It doesn't seem as if there's much good news these days. The stock market and the price of gold goes up one day and down the next. The dollar isn't doing very well against foreign currencies. The only things on the rise are drug and alcohol addiction. A couple of weeks of watching TV and you'll be a good candidate for drug or alcohol abuse yourself.

Is it any wonder some people don't enjoy retirement? They let themselves get into a rut and don't crank up their sights and shoot for the moon. Putting it in perspective, they choose instead to shoot straight ahead, hoping to hit the barn door—just so they can hold on to what they have. Or in some cases, they don't shoot at all. The problem is if they shoot at the barn door and miss, they end up in the barnyard. And back home where I come from the barnyard is filled with manure.

Real Winners Set Goals

Real winners are people who set and meet big goals, dream big dreams, achieve high hopes, and shoot for the moon. They're people who acknowledge world problems but don't succumb to them in their own lives. Successful people not only set goals, they also commit them to writing! Real winners don't choose the easiest goals possible. They seek out the more difficult goals—both for the pride they feel when the goals are reached and for the feeling of self-satisfaction they have in working toward those goals.

My father always told me things that are given to you or that you acquire without any effort are not appreciated. What I'm trying to get across is that a "goal" that can be accomplished without really working for it doesn't really deserve to be called a goal.

Successful people not only set big goals, they set them in five-year increments. They pick five years because goals that fit a shorter time frame seem less exciting and challenging. Now you might say, "Hey! I'm over 65 now. Don't you think that's a little optimistic to set a date past 70 for completion of the goal? After all, some people never make it to 70."

So, what do you want to do? Do you want to give up and throw in the towel? I'd rather be like George Burns and have a contract to appear in Las Vegas on my 100th birthday.

Your retirement goals will surely be different from those you had before you retired. You're the boss now. You have more time available to spend on those projects you couldn't touch before you retired. All that time spent commuting to and from work and that 40 to 60 hours per week that you worked—all that is yours now. So, now is the time to get off by yourself again and set the goals for accomplishing those things you have already decided you wanted to do in your retirement—and some other goals, too.

We're going to ask you to write down your personal goals; your professional goals; your mental goals; your physical goals; and your spiritual goals. Our reason for doing this is, for most people, goals and needs in these areas change after retirement.

As you think this through, I'm sure you will have some goals that surprise even you. And there might be some goals that don't specifically relate to the activity you've already decided on as your retirement activity. Write down all your goals, following the outlines included at the end of this chapter.

Decide what approach you want to take toward the activities you want to be doing. If it's a business you want to be in, should you start small and establish your own business or should you buy an exisiting business? What amount of money can you invest? How much money can you have flowing through the till for start-up expenses? How soon do you project a profit? Goals that will help answer these questions, and more, are necessary if you're going into business.

You also need goals to help you decide what you're going to do with your life as it relates to your family. What spiritual, mental, and physical activities are important to you? Decide those things right now and write them down on the pages provided at the end of this chapter. The first step in setting meaningful goals is to express them as clearly as you can and then WRITE THEM DOWN.

Proof That It Works

Just in case you think writing your goals down isn't all that important, I'm here to tell you you're wrong and I can prove it.

A few years ago, a behavioral research team from the prestigious Harvard Business School took a random sample of 100 graduating seniors and asked this question: "Where would you like to be and what would you like to be doing ten years from now?"

Every one of those 100 graduating seniors told the researchers they wanted to be rich and famous. They wanted to be doing important things, such as running big companies or in some way affecting and controlling the world we live in. The researchers weren't surprised by the answers they got. Harvard teaches their students they're exceptional and destined to lead. And they are, to some extent, for no other reason than the fact they've been to Harvard.

But even among those elite future leaders, something astonishing showed up. Among the 100 students questioned, ten young tigers not only wanted and expected to shape the world, but they had actually written clear goals describing what they wanted to accomplish and when. None of the other graduates had written down their goals.

Ten years later, the same researchers went back to those 100 graduates with an extensive survey. They found the ten students who had originally written down their goals and plans owned 96 percent of the total wealth of the entire 100 student sample. That means those ten graduates were virtually ten times more successful than their classmates.

Wow! We might have expected 30 percent, which is three times better, or maybe 50 percent. But 96 percent! That's truly amazing. And, gentle readers, with that revelation and proof, I rest my case for the vital importance of writing down goals.

As you write your goals, keep in mind that most goals or projects have a definite completion point. Pick a date for reaching that point.

By the Yard It's Hard,
. . . by the Inch It's a Cinch

Once you've written down your five-year goals and are committed to them, the next steps are remarkably simple. So take plenty of time with the five-year goals. They have to come first. They're the key to successful application. "By the yard it's hard, by the inch it's a cinch," pretty much says it all.

The key to meeting success with your big five-year goals is to simply cut them up into bite-sized day-by-day "do-ables." Here's how it works.

1. Once your five-year goals have been established, divide them by five. When you divide five-year goals by five, you end up with, what else—five one-year goals. When you establish your one-year goals, you should know exactly what you should do between now and this time next year.

2. Divide your yearly goals by twelve. Congratulations. You now have your month-by-month goals. You now know what you have to accomplish between now and this time next month if you're going to be on schedule with your five-year plan.

3. Divide your monthly goals by four. Couldn't fool you, could I? You knew this was coming. But, all kidding aside, you now know what you have to get started on next Monday morning. Just so you have no doubt about the entire process, go on to the next step.

4. Divide your weekly goals by 4, 5, 6, or 7. The number you pick depends completely on you and the number of days a week you want to devote to attaining your goals. If you love seven-day weeks, divide by seven. If you believe five is fine, divide by five. The number is up to you, but whatever you choose, the end product is the answer to that very tough question. "What do I need to do today in order to achieve my goal on schedule." When I think of schedules and time restrictions, I always think of one of the favorite sayings used by my friend, Kevin O'Sullivan. I've heard him say, when faced with a tight schedule, "Some things take longer than they do."

When you've followed this procedure through to the end, you'll be ready every morning to hit the deck running, with your target firmly fixed. You'll be ready to follow your own yellow brick road of daily, weekly, and monthly goals to the Emerald City of your fondest dreams. You'll find this works, whether you're building a boat, planning a trip around the world, starting your own business, or going to work for someone else.

Clearly stated daily, weekly, monthly, and yearly goals help you harness your personal power, focus your energy, and concentrate your effort on things you've decided will lead to the happiness and success you want out of your retirement. Developing small, manageable, day-to-day goals relieves you of the anxiety that comes from continually questioning what you're doing.

If you constantly doubt what you're doing, you'll always end up doing it poorly. But when you know what you're doing represents the best use of your time, you do it faster, better, and with more enthusiasm.

Setting five-year goals and dividing them into day-to-day do-ables can also surprise you. The process can help you to determine whether you're really shooting for the moon or just aiming at the half moon carved on the outhouse door.

Say, for example, you've taken a retirement job that involves selling and in this example you're working five days a week. Let's say you've set a goal of 500 new sales contacts a year in order to meet your dollar goals. As you schedule your working days, taking out all the holidays, you'll find there are approximately 250 working days when you'll be calling on customers. That's just two calls a day. You're going to say to yourself, "Hey! I can do better than that."

You're going to say, "I can do a heck of a lot better than two calls a day. Just watch me." And soon you're going to increase that goal of 500 calls per year because you know you can do it.

That's exactly what happened to me. I found I could do my five-day weekly plan in three and a half days. So, by the end of the third month, I was working on my fifth month. The act of setting my day-to-day five-year goals took the mystery out of success and turned magic into movement.

Just remember the bottom line. *By the yard it's hard, by the inch it's a cinch.* The key to success is to write down those goals and use them as guideposts and mileage markers for your journey to success.

Keep It Visible

If you write down your goals and file them away, they aren't worth the paper they're written on. You have to keep the goals alive in your day-to-day life. As I have found so many times in my life, after many painful lessons, you have to keep your eyes on the goal and to focus on taking the steps that get you to your destination.

One such specific occasion comes to mind for me. During my formative years, I created the dream and set the goal of being a millionaire by the time I was 30 years old. I was so cock sure about it that I was even giving advice to my friends about financial success.

Then one day the moment of truth arrived—my thirtieth birthday. As I lay there in bed that morning, I was faced with the hard cold truth. I was not only not a millionaire, I was about $1,015,000 behind my goal. I owed on my car, furniture, TV, appliances, etc. I was crushed.

After several weeks of "thumb sucking" and blaming my missed-fortune on everyone but myself, I had the courage to look back and try to determine why and how I screwed up.

In reviewing the formula's used by the great "Horatio Alger" folk heros I had studied in my quest for success, I realized I had carelessly skipped over one of the most crucial and important aspects of achieving success. Keeping it visible!

So, after a lot of soul searching, I was still sure I wanted to be a millionaire. But I was embarrassed by the big deal I made of being a shoo-in by age 30 and then missing it. So I cautiously wrote down 39 as my new target for becoming a millionaire. To help me keep it visible and remember what I was trying to accomplish, I did what I now feel in hindsight was the turning point for me.

I took a 1922 silver dollar I had been carrying around as a good luck piece and put my great big goal on it. That's right. I took it down to my basement workbench, put it in a vise, and used emery cloth to polish off the reverse side and prepare it for inscription. Then I took it to a jeweler and had him engrave these words: *I will be a millionaire when I am 39.*

The jeweler must have believed me, because I think he overcharged me for the job. Even if he had charged me a quarter of a million, it would have been a worthwhile investment because my profit margin would still have been three quarters of a million dollars.

I won't try to tell you that every morning when I scooped my change and keys off the dresser I looked at the silver dollar and gave myself a pep talk about getting out there and doing the day's duty. That would be a lie. But I can tell you there were many days when I was down and willing to take some time off and start next week. There were times I wanted the day to end with lunch, but I kept on going because of that silver dollar with a simple but awesome goal engraved on it.

I can vividly remember digging into my pocket for telephone change or lunch money and coming up with that silver dollar. I didn't always stop to read it aloud, but consciously and subconsciously it always reminded me of the minimum progress I had to achieve every day.

I'm convinced that on more than one or two occasions that little reminder kept me doing what had to be done. With God as my witness, I'm telling you I never missed doing what I had to do each and every day, just the way I had planned it.

I retired that 1922 silver dollar on my 35th birthday— four years ahead of schedule.

There it is! You've heard my story. You know in your heart that goal setting works. The behavioral scientists know from their research that goal setting works. And I know that goal setting works because it worked for me in my life when nothing else did. So don't procrastinate—DO IT! Not just because I suggested it or because it has worked so well for others. DO IT FOR YOURSELF.

Remember that a meaningful objective is one that will communicate your intent to accomplish something by a certain time. The objective can be described in dollars or something you will be doing—a degree or award you will receive, a project you will complete, or even how much you will weigh by a certain date. There's always a quantity or a specific achievement included in the goal.

You may use the outlines found on the next few pages to record your goals. Some retirees find the space on each page too cramped and prefer to set up their goals on separate sheets of paper. Actually, the separate sheets are better in some ways, since you'll need additional sheets as the weeks and months roll by.

My Five Year Goals

Five years from now   . . . . 19 . . . . .

Personal Goals

Professional Goals

Mental Goals

Physical Goals

Spiritual Goals

One Year From Now . . . . . . 19 . . . . .

Personal Goals

Professional Goals

Mental Goals

Physical Goals

Spiritual Goals

One Month from Now . . . . . 19 . . . . .

Personal goals

Professional goals

Mental goals

Physical goals

Spiritual goals

One Week from Now . . . . 19 . . .

Personal goals

Professional goals

Mental goals

Physical goals

Spiritual goals

Tomorrow and Everyday from Now On

Personal goals

Professional goals

Mental goals

Physical goals

Spiritual goals

Additional Notes to Myself on Goal Setting

S^{TEP} F^{OUR}

WORK OR ACTIVITY?

If you'll take a moment to look over the preceding chapters, you'll notice we've made a lot of promises. We promised to share everything we've learned about success and retirement. We promised if you took time to find your fastball, you'd have a critical weapon to make your retirement successful and productive. We promised if you'd pick your opportunities and set big motivating goals, you'd be ahead of the game.

But there's one thing we didn't promise. We didn't say it would be easy—especially if you want to emulate Colonel Sanders in your retirement. Not on your life! Because intrinsic to every big accomplishment, implied in every goal, is a very unpopular four letter word—WORK!

There's only one place where success comes before work, and that's in the dictionary.

You may be a certified genius with an IQ of 700. You may be president of your local Mensa chapter. You may be as glib as Gielgud. But to be successful in meeting your goals, actualizing your plans, and fulfilling your dreams, you have to get out and boogie. You have to work!

Now we know that this isn't a popular piece of advice, not today in the age of expected entitlements. The simple fact is that without the lubrication of elbow grease and a dose of the old-fashioned work ethic, the machinery of success is going to grind to a complete halt.

If you're planning to seek employment with a large corporation, you should know that, according to a recent survey, less than a third of the top executives in the firms surveyed support flexible or reduced working schedules for older workers. It's not a pretty picture, but things are changing.

By the end of the century, there will be 21 million new jobs created. At the same time, there will be 15 million fewer employees in the 19 to 25 age bracket. The age of the baby boomers is passing. Employers are beginning to realize this. Soon, the need for senior employees will become critical. Some companies are already in the process of changing personnel policies in order to keep older, valuable employees and to allow the hiring of senior employees on a part-time basis.

But let's be realistic. The majority of personnel managers you will contact have a fixed and firm belief that older workers have outdated skills, that they're inflexible and that they're lacking in motivation. It will be your challenge to convince them you're indeed flexible, motivated, and positive, and your lifetime of experience will be an asset to the company.

Another thing we have to deal with as we make contacts is the notion that retired folks are slower to learn, absent more often, etc. There is empirical evidence that a worker's performance does not decline with age, that their absence rates are much lower than for younger workers, and that they learn at least as rapidly as younger workers. Also, older workers have fewer occupational accidents, lower personnel turnover, and higher morale.

What about health? In fact, we're healthier today than anyone our age has ever been—because we're better informed and because of the advances in medical science. It's a known fact that many people have improved health after retirement. This could be because we have more time to take care of ourselves. But our health won't improve if all we do is sit in front of the TV set.

Goofing Off

For many people, "goofing off" has become a way of life in retirement. It's an entitlement that those people have come to expect. They expect it because they did, in fact, "goof off" during the last years of their working life. Ask them what work was like before retirement, and they'll tell you it was dull and boring. Ask what their retirement is like, and they'll tell you it's great! Now, who's kidding whom? Their retirement life's dull and boring, too, but they just won't admit it.

In a 1982 essay, Robert Half, the employment specialist, said "goofing off" is literally goofing up the American economy. Time thefts deal a severe blow to the nation's productivity. They also fuel inflation by raising the cost of goods and services.

Half came to this conclusion after asking 312 firms to estimate the amount of time stolen by their employees every week. Using their figures, he arrived at a weekly average of 4.3 hours per employee. He multiplied this by the average hourly rate of $7.41 and came up with $31.86 per employee per week as the actual per person cost of "goofing off."

Then Half multiplied the per employee "goof off" cost by the number of non-agricultural, private-sector jobs in the U.S. He came up with a whopping $120 BILLION as the cost of goofing off each year. That's more than the cost of all shoplifting, fraud, and criminal acts committed against the private sector in the year preceding this study. And remember these are 1981 dollars we're talking about.

Goofing off is an insidious problem. It's found in taking a longer lunch hour, leaving early and coming late, jawing with fellow employees for a minute or two, or taking a phony sick day. No big deal you say? Wrong! Wrong! Wrong! It's a $120 billion rip-off, and it can keep you from meeting your goals and dreams. You have to do what needs to be done to meet your goals and dreams. No goofing off!

What is Work?

Since we're so unyielding in our belief that you should not goof off and one obvious alternative to goofing off is to work, perhaps we should redefine what we mean by work.

The dictionary says that work is exertion directed to produce or accomplish something and then goes on to describe work in many different ways.

There's more space devoted to the description of work in the dictionary than to almost any other word. There must be a reason for that. Perhaps most people don't understand what work really is.

We like one description of work that was included in Studs Terkel's book titled *Work*. It's a quote from Ralph Helstein, who was president emeritus of the United Packinghouse Workers of America when the book was written. Mr. Helstein's description of work is as follows:

"Learning is work. Caring for children is work. Community action is work. Once we accept the concept of work as something meaningful, not just as the source of a buck, you don't have to worry about finding enough jobs. There's no excuse for mules any more. Society does not need them. There's no question about our ability to feed and clothe and house everybody. The problem is going to come in finding enough ways for a man to keep occupied, so he's in touch with reality."

Our imaginations have obviously not yet been challenged.

So, when we refer to "work," we include all that's named above and more.

Press On

I'm fond of an old adage entitled "Press On." I've attributed it to everyone from Abraham Lincoln to Herbert Hoover, so I'm not sure where the credit really belongs. It's still a splendid summary of my feelings about success and effort. It goes like this:

> *"Nothing in the world can take*
> *the place of persistence.*
> *Talent will not;*
> *nothing is more common than*
> *unsuccessful people with talent.*
> *Genius will not;*
> *unrewarded genius is almost a proverb.*
> *Education will not;*
> *the world is full of educated derelicts.*
> *Persistence and determination alone*
> *are omnipotent."*

I admit it's possible to have the good things in life without doing a lot of work. You might inherit a bundle. You could win the million dollar lottery. You could hit on a big dollar slot machine. You could marry rich. You could simply luck-out. Some people do. But considering the odds, I wouldn't plan on it for the first thing Monday morning.

The fact is I haven't found a way to make it sweat-free. And I haven't heard of anybody else who has either. For me, and for everyone else who's made a success of life, hard work is what has done it.

Now, there are some who have worked for years and reach retirement with a combination of money from profit sharing funds, IRA's, monthly retirement checks from one or two sources, and their life savings. These people have paid their dues. They're entitled to have some of the good things in life without additional "work," as most people think of it. But for their own good health, peace of mind, marital bliss, and general self-esteem, they should be involved in some of the types of "work" we call community service if they don't want to become involved in a paying job.

Many Americans have this odd, unrealistic, image of their rights and entitlements. Like a field of Aesop's fabled grasshoppers, they sing: "The world owes me a living."

You remember the entire fable don't you? The ant had stored away kernels of wheat, which he had gathered during the summer to tide him over the coming winter. One frosty autumn day, a grasshopper, half perishing from hunger, came limping by. He asked for a morsel from the ant's store to save his life. "What were you doing all summer while I was busy harvesting?" inquired the ant. "Oh," replied the grasshopper, "I was not idle. I was singing and chirping all day long." "Well," said the ant grimly as he locked his granary door, "since you sang all summer, it looks as though you would have to dance all winter."

Success to me is not an easy street. Success to me isn't nine-to-five for 35 years and then out to pasture. Success to me isn't a risk-free, worry-free, perspiration-free way of life. There are so many ways to measure success that it can be confusing. One thing I know is that you can't measure success on a scale of one to ten. I like Booker T. Washington's definition. He said, "Success is to be measured, not so much by the position one has achieved in life, as by the obstacles he has overcome while trying to succeed." John Foster Dulles put it another way. "The measure of success," he said, "is not whether you have a tough problem to deal with, but whether it's the same problem you had last year."

The Importance of Work

To me, work and achievement are irrevocably linked in a process that continues after most people quit their jobs at 5 o'clock. And it continues right through the weekends. If you're doing something that will contribute to the success of a project, don't stop just because it's 5 o'clock.

Unfortunately, we've been so indoctrinated by the 8-to-5, 40-hour standard work week or the 9-to-5, 35-hour week, we don't even realize there are other options. It's in those hours after 5 o'clock that success slips away from us. The few hours we spend after 5 o'clock to complete a project can be the difference between success and failure. And there's always a lot of wasted effort when you're trying to "put together the pieces" the next morning.

It was my practice to ignore the clock before retirement, and it's my practice now. I believe that even in retirement we must have our goals and work to achieve them. If you aren't looking forward to work and accomplishments as long as you last, then you're just sitting there going to seed.

I came across a *Twin Cities Magazine* article about Charles Tesar, a man who had become exceptionally successful in the retail jewelry business. George immigrated to the United States from German-occupied Europe after World War II. He started from scratch and made extraordinary progress by any standards. This is what the article quotes him as saying.

"There is gold in them thar hills [America]," said George. "Anything that someone wants to do can become a success story. There is big competition in America from nine to five. But, before nine and after five, there is no competition. People go home. If you work later or give a little more than you expect to get back immediately, you can't help but win in America because so many people stand with their hands out saying 'Gimmie, gimmie, gimmie.' They don't come and ask, 'What can I do for you, boss?' or "What more can I do?'"

In my scheme of things, success and work are synonymous. Work isn't something to be avoided. It's something to identify with. I equate work with the nobility of achievement. Work is the process part of success. Success is both the journey and the destination, and work is the activity of succeeding. If your work is to succeed, you must have a sense of success in it. Work is the critical difference between wishing and winning.

Work is Something Meaningful

I need to remind myself, and you, that when I speak of work in this chapter I'm also speaking about any retirement activity you may be involved in. Remember the description of work that appeared early in this chapter? Learning is work. Caring for children is work. Community action is work. Work is something meaningful, not just the source of a buck.

One of our first stated objectives for this book was that whatever the circumstances of your retirement may be, we want to inspire you to get up from that chair and DO SOMETHING. We didn't say it in those exact words, but what we've been trying to tell you all along is that inactivity can cause serious health and mental problems. And we haven't even touched on the mental part of it. Life can be pretty dull when you're just sitting there doing nothing. A person who lets his or her mind stagnate by not being involved in projects where the mind must be used is apt to become forgetful at a much younger age than a person who is involved in mind-stretching activities on a regular basis. Psychologists tell us that people who sit around with nothing to do are more likely to become alcoholics than people who have a busy life-style.

If the dreams you're dreaming, the goals you're setting, and the plans you're making aren't as exciting to think about as a weekend golf game or tennis match or as lovely and warming to think of as your family and friends, then you may not have done as good a goal-setting job as you could. It's going to take a lot of concentration, a lot of time and a lot of hard work to reach the goal you set for yourself when you saw your mountain, set your goals, and wrote your objectives.

You know you've got to be the right person in the right place at the right time and do everything the right way. So you'd better love that dream of yours. You're going to have to eat with it, sleep with it, and live with it 24 hours a day, every day of the week. Harold Cummings, chairman emeritus of Minnesota Mutual, gives this advice on work. "If you want to leave your footprints in the sands of time, make sure you're wearing your work boots."

I hope you don't think I'm a killjoy, trying to convince you that success comes from slavish drudgery in service to neurotic goals. Remember, you're retired now. If you've followed my instructions, you've chosen your "fastball," something you like to do. When you're doing something you like, work isn't all that bad. So what I'm trying to do is dispel from your mind that unruffled, cool-countenance image of success that the deodorant and hairspray commercials serve up.

I'm sure you've seen the television images of success. The heroes are usually seen lying in the sun, sipping something cool, while making big deals on the phone. They're also seen swishing silently down Wall Street in chauffered limousines, buying and selling companies and countries. These simple-minded scenarios make beautiful commercials, but they're as off base as they are glamorous.

This is not to belittle the pleasures of travel. I'm just telling you the commercial image of success is not realistic. If one of your retirement goals is to travel extensively, I think that's great. It will get you away from the TV. It will broaden your interests. You won't become a couch potato. I'm not opposed to that kind of a goal for a retiree, if you can afford it. But take it from one who knows. There's a lot of work connected with world travel if you do the planning.

Not long ago, an old friend from Greenwich, Connecticut, was in town and stopped by our home. We chatted and caught up on what had happened since we last saw each other. Then my friend got up, looked around our home, and with a great deal of enthusiasm said, "Hauser, you're the luckiest guy I've ever known. Everything always works out fabulously well for you."

After saying that, my friend walked over and gave me a warm pat on the back. Well, I really appreciated the warmth, sincerity, and enthusiasm with which that compliment was paid to me. I responded with a big "thanks" and a warm handshake.

I thought about those comments after we parted. Then I smiled to myself and thought how true the old saying is: "The harder I work, the luckier I get." By many standards, I'm very lucky. But by many standards, I'm a darn hard worker. I internalize what I've been telling you in this book. Then I go out and put all the principles into action. I pour on whatever energy, work, perspiration, or combination thereof it takes to make things turn out the way I want them to. I suppose I should have reminded my friend that luck comes to those who are ready for it. Of course I'm lucky, but it takes a lot of work to get ready to be lucky.

I figure if I give a 100 percent effort I will have the best chance of success—and I'll be successful more often than not. It's just not in me to give something a 50 or 60 percent effort, because I know that kind of effort is doomed to failure. And if you know you've given 100 percent and still fail, don't give up. The experience you gain from that failure may be just what you need to be successful on the next try.

Workaholics

"Workaholic" is a fairly new word used to denote someone addicted to work. Yet others have felt the same way we do about success. Thomas Edison, who was known for his ability to work hard for days on end, was neither dull nor poor. He had this to say about work and success. "I never did anything worth doing by accident, nor did any of my inventions come by chance. They came by work." Edison also said, "Show me a satisfied man, and I will show you a failure."

In his lifetime, Edison was one of the most successful and fun-loving people to be found. But he also was one of the hardest workers.

Benjamin Franklin, America's first certified genius, was well known for hard work, hard play, and a goodly measure of success. He also had a way with words. His alter-ego, Poor Richard, had this to say about success. "In order to succeed, you have to handle your tools with mittens."

Franklin was a versatile man. He discovered electricity in lightning and developed the lightning rod. He experimented with eyeglasses and developed the bifocal lens. He invented the potbelly stove, which people to this day call the "Franklin Stove." He established the first post office, the first lending library, the first life insurance. And he wrote the world's first self-help success book, *Poor Richard's Almanac*. He did all these things and at the same time he printed a newspaper and was involved in the political affairs of our new country. Ben Franklin clearly believed in work and fun.

Today, people who are eager to succeed, like you and me and Franklin and Edison, are called workaholics. The term surfaced in the indulgent sixties to give comfort to those who felt the world owed them the lifelong option of sniffing the daisies, chasing butterflies, and baying at the moon.

You remember that period in the 1960's. The Zonker Harrises of our society said it was beneath their dignity to dedicate themselves to a cause as mundane and potentially insensitive as working for some profit-making organization. They felt it was OK to go to school forever, if old Dad would foot the bill. They felt it was their mission in life to always be involved in the most fashionable social cause—as long as it didn't take too much effort on their part. They spent a lot of time suffering some existential anxiety known as "trying to get one's head together."

They also felt it was OK to simply do nothing. What was not socially acceptable was to enthusiastically spend one's time and energy in a commercial effort. Those who did were branded workaholics. They were considered low-brows and were looked upon as being neurotic, if not actually psychotic.

A few years ago, Dr. Marilyn Machlowitz wrote a book called *Workaholics*. It was based on her Ph.D. dissertation and a series of articles she'd done for the New York Times. Her subjects were people who were considered workaholics.

Her findings surprised a lot of people. She found workaholics are people who work a lot, like what they're doing, and enjoy using the tools of their trade. She found no evidence to indicate hard working people are psychological deviates who are automatically prone to "type A" behavior, stress-related illnesses, or heart disease. Like my father always said, "Hard work never hurt anybody."

Eugene Jennings, a management professor at Michigan State University did a similar study of highly successful executives. He asked each of them if they were happy. Those who answered "yes" were those who generally worked 60 hours a week or more. But not only were those executives happy, they were also free of alcoholism and didn't have an unusually high divorce rate.

I don't think the problem lies with the so-called workaholic—the person for whom an hour of work seems like fifteen minutes, who honestly enjoys what he or she is doing, or who feels the way Betty Rollin did when she wrote her book *Am I Really Getting Paid for This?* To me, it seems the problem lies with the people who call the eager beavers "kooks" and who rationalize their own discomfort, boredom, and lack of accomplishment by labeling the hard worker a kook, neurotic, workaholic, brown-noser, company stooge, or dozens of other derogatory and degrading names, including some that are unprintable.

So the next time you hear yourself being called a name because you're working hard, consider it a compliment and remember the workaholic is a rare and lucky individual.

Self-Motivation

Self-motivation: That's one of the most important messages in this book. Everything we've been talking about is aimed at self-motivation. Before you retired, there was always the "boss" to keep you moving toward the company goals.

Now it's up to you, and if you've followed our instructions up to this point, you've already moved up several steps toward the "best years of your life."

You've found your fastball. You know your strengths, your talents, and things you like to do. You also know your weaknesses and things you're not very good at and don't like to do. You've looked at your before-retirement job and hobbies and decided which after-retirment job or activity will best suit your retirement life-style.

Also, you've done a cost estimate of what your chosen retirement job or activity might cost you. You've listed the people who might help you, and you've set your goals for what you want to accomplish in five years, one year, one month, and next week. Now, aren't all of those tools for self-motivation?

I've heard very few people say they don't like retirement. These are truly "the best years of your life." You've heard about Hippies and Yuppies. We, they now have a name for us. They call us Sippies, which stands for Senior Independent Proprietors. That's not a bad description for most of us. We can't deny we're Senior. The Social Security income, our life's savings, and retirement benefits, along with paid-up mortgages, allow us to be "independent." We just don't want to become so independent that we lose all incentive to do things and end up being couch potatoes.

The Universal Law of Reciprocity we talked about earlier states that to the extent we give others what they're looking for, they will, in turn, give us what we're looking for. But you have to give them what they want first. Think of how that law applies to some of the volunteer work you might have set as your goal. To quote Henry Wadsworth Longfellow, "Give what you have. To someone, it may be better than you dare to think."

The application of the Universal Law of Recriprocity in employee motivation is well known, especially by psychologists such as Dr. David Berlow. About employee motivation, Dr. Berlow says, "I only know three things about motivation. Find out what the employee wants. Figure out how to get what you want through his getting what he wants, and then work like hell to see that he gets what he wants."

That formula applies to us in retirement as well as it applies to employee motivation. The formula works both ways. To get what you want, figure out what the other person wants. Decide how you can get what you want from their getting what they want, and then work like hell to see that they get what they want. Remember the law—because it's important. To the extent you give others what they want, they in turn will give you what you want. And to get the best results, you have to work hard at giving others what they want, and you have to give them what they want first.

A Final Word About Work and Other Retirement Activities

Work is a direct investment. When you stop working, the return on your investment dries up. I've been retired for six years now, and I haven't stopped working. That doesn't mean I get paid for everything I do. On the contrary, the major part of my work is directed toward projects that help other people—without my getting paid for it. I've headed at least five fund drives. I'm a member of two civic boards. I'm still active in two professinal organizations. For several years, I served as the U.S. Representative for an international training organization (IFTDO). And I wasn't paid for any of those services. That doesn't mean I did not get some returns in the form of prestige, self-satisfaction, friendship, and many other non-monetary rewards.

I suppose what I'm trying to do is take you back again to the definition of work we discussed at the beginning of this step. "Learning is work. Caring for children is work. Community action is work. Once you accept the concept of work as something meaningful, not just the source of a buck, you don't have to worry about jobs."

Using that definition of work as doing something meaningful, you can find me working in my office, located in my home, every day I'm home. Now that doesn't mean I don't take time to keep my body in shape. Also, it doesn't mean I don't travel. I spend two months in Florida each year and travel to other points in the U.S. and Canada more often than the average person. I've been to China twice since I retired—once as a delegation leader for an exchange group. I also led an exchange group to the Soviet Union and have visited many of the European countries twice since my retirement.

I'm thoroughly convinced you have to use it or you'll lose it, and now I'm speaking about your brain. I've seen it happen time after time where a person seemingly grows years older shortly after they retire. When you check into the problem, you find they have grown stale and stagnant. They're no longer stretching their brain, so it literally shrivels up like a prune. The same concept goes for your body. It takes work and motivation to keep your mind and body fit.

Full Speed Ahead

If you leave here and start experiencing some success toward reaching your goals, you're going to have to be very careful about retaining your motivation and your commitment. The early victories, the first breath of success, and the pats on the back from your family and friends can be seductive. Those good feelings can cause you to lay back and start living it up, and then you can get into trouble. It's easy to mislead yourself into believing you don't have to keep pumping the handle to keep the successes coming. You have to keep pumping if the trickle of success is to ever become a stream.

Another seduction is the lure of the fast buck. Most retired persons can't afford to become involved in fast buck schemes. There's always a high risk in that kind of plan. And, when you present the image of a successful retired person, people will come to you with all kinds of hot tips and inside information. Every one of these favors will end up with an appeal for cash. Don't be tempted by the illusion that the "big guys" do it with mirrors and magic and not with hard work.

"I like your style," say the leeches. "And I'm going to help you make it really big. We'll put your money in fandangos, pal, and then we'll really go places together." Just remember when you start experiencing success, that's the time to double your effort and put the pedal to the metal. It's not time to take your foot off the gas and start reading Burma Shave signs.

Do you remember Andrew Carnegie's favorite piece of advice? He said, "Put all of your eggs in one basket—

and then watch that basket."

One of my favorite axioms is, "Very often, when people become successful, they stop doing the very things that made them successful in the first place."

Work or activity is what we're talking about here. Plan on it. Respect it. And never be seduced into thinking it is your genius or talent or good looks that got you where you are when success begins to come your way. Attribute it to the hard work and muscle you put behind your fastball.

People will tell you you've earned a rest. They'll say you're retired now and deserve to goof off and take it easy. Depending on your financial situation, sometimes that may be true. There's a difference between working to live and living to work. In our retirement we look at work in a different way. It's the activity that keeps up our interest in life. It keeps our minds active and our hearts young. Our goals, as we pointed out earlier, should reflect this difference in our retirement life-style.

Have you noticed how the unsuccessful people say, "Thank God it's Friday," while the successful people say, "Oh God, it can't be Friday already." Or, as Paul Harvey said at age 70 as he celebrated his fortieth anniversary of broadcasting on radio and TV, "I would retire tomorrow if someone could figure out something else to do that was more fun than this." It's obvious that successful and unsuccessful people have different dreams and goals and march to the sound of different drummers.

Take Paul Newman for example. At age 63 he opened a camp in Ashford, Connecticut, for youngsters with cancer or other life-threatening diseases. Paul hit on the idea when two of his close friends died after long bouts with cancer.

The cost to build and endow the project was $17 million. That's no small project. But, without fanfare or a great amount of publicity, Paul set out to get the funding. The first money donated came from Newman's Own, the firm that produces salad dressing, popcorn, lemonade, and spaghetti sauce. The firm has donated $15 million to 350 charities in the last five years. It contributed $7 million to this project. Then Newman went out to get other donations.

A visit to a 25-year-old Saudi businessman, who now lives in Washington, D.C., and has suffered from an inherited blood disease that has required hospitalization every three weeks since childhood, opened the door for another large donation. Five days after Paul's meeting with the Saudi businessman, he received a check for $5 million from King Fahd. "I never expected it," Newman says. In addition to the $5 million donation, Newman also received donations from corporations and individuals.

Newman named the camp the "Hole in the Wall Gang Camp." The children who go there are not regimented. Although the camp is equipped with wheelchairs and medical facilities and the kids who go there have cancer, leukemia, histiocytosis, aplastic anemia, thalassemia, and other disorders, this is the least regimented camp one can imagine. "I want to get the kids away from regulations," Newman said.

Now, why do you think we included this story about Paul Newman? Well, here's a man who has enough money to retire and do nothing except fish or play golf or race cars for the rest of his life. Instead he chooses to become involved in a project for kids with life-threatening diseases. A big chunk of the money came from his own company. He turned a hobby into a profit-making operation, but since he doesn't need the money, profits from the company are assigned to charity. "The trick of living," he says, "is to slip on and off the planet with the least fuss you can muster. I'm not running for sainthood. I just happen to think that in life we need to be a little like the farmer who puts back into the soil some of what he takes out."

Every Day a New Challenge

Every day of our retirement can bring a new challenge. Each day can be another interesting day to wake up to. You're not put out to pasture when you retire—unless you want to be put there. Renew your zeal for your goals. Gather your faith and build your strength every time you pitch your fastball. Don't apologize or feel sheepish about a little perspiration. It's the daily testament, the hourly medal, and the vivid proof that every day, in every way, you're doing a little bit better and taking another step toward reaching your goal.

There's just one more story about what you can do with your time in retirement and then a little advice before we leave this chapter. I want to tell you about H. J. "Jack" Post, who was a friend of mine for many years.

Jack was a big, red-headed man. His hands were huge, and you knew it when he shook hands with you.

Jack is dead now, but before he died, he wrote a book called *How You Can Be What You Want to Be*. I have a copy of the book, because I was one of the people who reviewed it before publication. The reason I want to tell this story about Jack is that he was about 70 years old before he wrote the book, and it was his first literary effort. Also, it was his retirement project, although Jack wouldn't admit until the day of his death that he was retired.

Jack was a true product of industry. He started working as a machinist for an Indiana auto parts plant in 1917. He advanced progressively, from machinist through various stages of supervision, until he became superintendent of the auto parts plant. I always pictured him in my mind as the typical "bull of the woods."

Jack was President of the National Management Association in 1942 and later served five years as Managing Director of that organization. He encouraged and procured acceptance of the idea that the Management Club is an essential part of any industrial organization. Later, in 1952, Jack established his own manufacturing company and eventually owned several small manufacturing companies.

When Jack came to a retirement age, he sold the companies but was retained in an advisory position. Half of his time was devoted to working for the National Management Association and for the Freedom Foundation. I must say Jack was one of the most memorable people I've ever known. There was never a dull moment in his life.

Work Hard—Don't Apologize

That's the end of my sermonette on work. It's the cleanest four-letter word in the English language. The rest is up to you. You've got to decide whether to run, throw, or punt. You need to choose whether to take up the challenge or look the other way. And if you believe, as I do, that the only place where success comes before work is in the dictionary, I'll make you this iron-clad promise. Work hard and you'll never have to apologize to anyone, especially the person you see in the bathroom mirror, for anything you get, any goals you reach, or any success you may earn.

Work hard at what you do, whether it's for your own pleasure in your retirement or for a civic benefit or a retirement business you're starting. Get out there and boogie, and you'll own the most important thing in life—the self-respect and dignity that comes from hard work. You'll also enjoy the inner peace that only comes from knowing you did it the best way possible: Your way.

There's a saying that the rung of a ladder was never meant to rest upon but only to hold a man's foot long enough to put the other one higher. But let's pause here at the fourth step on your way to the "best years of your life" and look at your work habits. Even in retirement, it behooves us to find the most efficient way of doing things. So let's spend some time looking objectively at our past habits and then spend a little time listing what we can do to improve them.

Again, I want you to remember our definition of work. Learning is work. Caring for children is work. Community action is work, etc.

Notes to Myself on Work

*Current work habits and techniques
I will continue to use.*

Notes to Myself on Work

*New work habits I will develop in
order to reach my goals.*

S**TEP** F**IVE**

HAVE FUN!

You're probably thinking, "Wait a minute! What are they trying to pull on me? Why a chapter on having fun after that stirring sermon on hard work? They have to be the last guys in the world who appreciate a good time."

Maybe *you* could skip this chapter, but it's short so read it anyway. You'd be surprised at how many people manage to live through their entire working life and reach retirement without a hobby and without any other outside interests that will keep them active. Their only interest in sports is to sit in front of the fire and watch the games on TV. They surely need to read this chapter more than you, but it's not written for them alone. It's written for everyone.

We didn't want you to get the feeling we're some sort of nuts who think if it hurts it must be good for you. Nothing could be farther from the truth. We see no contradiction in the way we feel about work and having fun. In fact, we think the two are logically connected. You've heard of the old adage, "Work hard and play hard," but our thoughts on the subject go deeper than that.

Do you remember what we said in Step One about cultivating a flower garden all your life? Now it's time to smell the roses. We said, "You can sell some. You can give some away, but for your own sake, do something with them."

Back there in Step One we asked you to make a list of the things that come easy for you—the things that are fun. We asked you to list things that were hobbies—that you never thought of as work. Some of those things should have filtered through into the list of things you're planning to do in "the best years of your life."

By this time, you should have your sights pretty well set on what you want to do in your retirement. Perhaps some of the pieces are already falling into place so you know you can achieve what you've planned. I'm like a kid in a candy store when I see my plans falling in place. I have a ball! I love it! If you don't have that feeling yet, keep working toward the goals you set. Follow the plan and the results will be there for you.

Once upon a time I really did think success had to hurt and be grim to be right. But I eventually found that while I had to think a little deeper, plan a little more carefully, and work a little harder to succeed, the payoff was just fantastic.

The same thing will happen to you. You'll find your life will never be the same, once things start working out for you. You'll go bananas when your Walter Mitty world becomes a reality. It's like being an astronaut on a trip to the moon. It's exhilarating. It's finding out that you're finally doing what you've wanted to do your whole life. My friend, nothing is more fun than that. I promise.

One of the biggest kicks I get is to sit back, look at my progress, and delight in my accomplishments. I'm having the time of my life, and I'm completely in charge of my fate. That might be a new experience for some of you who were tied into a job you didn't like before retirement. You had to respond to the dictates of a boss who didn't always make the best use of your talents. Now it's yours to savour while you do the things you can do best—while you pitch your fastball.

The Fun of Success

There's an extra benefit in being a success. Successful people live longer than other people. That's what the medical scientists tell us. Add to that the fact that retirees, as a group, are healthier than "working" people their same age and you have a double whammy. You have an excellent chance of living a long life.

There are several reasons for this. Successful people, especially retirees, don't suffer from depression and anxiety day in and day out. They don't sit around anesthetizing themselves with booze and pills to hide from the jobs they don't like. They don't burn themselves out by living a life full of anxiety and fear. They're their own boss and can set their own schedules.

Henry Ford lived into his nineties. Grandma Moses was 78 years old when she began to paint. She was still painting when she was 100. She died in 1962, shortly before she reached her 102nd birthday.

Albert Schweitzer, born in 1875, was still operating his hospital in the territory that had been French Equatorial Africa when he died in 1965. Schweitzer's philosophy was, "In gratitude for your own good fortune, you must in return render some sacrifice of your life for other life."

Arthur Rubenstein died at the age of 93. Actually he was just about a month short of his 94th birthday. Rubenstein was busy at his work almost until the day of his death. And perhaps you're familiar with the works of Marc Chagall, the famous contemporary painter. On his 95th birthday, July 7, 1982, when asked his personal motto for happiness, he said: "Work, work, and more work." According to his wife, Valentina, Chagall spent most of his time working on his paintings, which is what he liked to do best.

Let's talk about some people who are very much alive at the time of this writing. First, what do you think about Irving Berlin. He was born on January 28, 1887. His 100th birthday celebration was a celebration for the whole nation because of the many patriotic songs he wrote. Yes, he slowed down a little, but his zest for life is still great.

And what about George Burns? George was born on January 20, 1896. He earned his first Oscar when he was 80 years old. He's over 90 now and going for 100. He even has a signed contract for appearing in Las Vegas on his 100th birthday.

Bob Hope is another well known individual who's well into his eighties and still going strong. Born May 29, 1903, Hope started his show business career in the 1920's. Anyone who has seen Bob stand before an audience for an hour, telling one joke after another, knows he's a man who loves his work.

At age 77, Sarah McClendon is a White House Correspondent. She's been there through the terms of nine presidents and plans to be there for several more. You've probably seen her at many press conferences over the years. If there's a tough question to be asked, she'll ask it. Sarah says, "We are the people's representatives looking at government. And by golly if we weren't doing it, it would be a hell of a lot worse than it is."

Successful people are exhiairated by the quest for success. They get so enthusiastic and excited that their whole metabolism changes. New plans and ideas pour out. As they move into a higher state of excitement, they develop a closer harmony between their work and their goals. They operate at a totally different level of energy and existence than the "9-to-5," "Thank God it's Friday," crowd. Successful people have found that to do something and do it well provides it's own rewards.

You're going to be surprised at how easily things fall into place once you start following the daily and weekly schedules you've set up for yourself. You'll get the work done that needs to be done. You can apply yourself fully to each task without worrying about the rest of the work because you know it's scheduled too. You can attack each task with more energy, more direction, and better concentration. You'll discover the continuing sense of fun and excitement that's spawned by your enthusiasm for what you're doing.

Time flies when you're doing what you're really good at and when you've having fun at your work. An hour doesn't seem like an hour. A day doesn't seem like a day. There have been many days when I was so intent on working on a project and enjoying it so much that I forgot to eat lunch. I wouldn't even realize I was skipping lunch until about dinner time. Every time I experience one of those days I can look back on it with a sense of accomplishment because I do my best creative work when I shut out the rest of the world. And I enjoy it the most!

Now It's Time for Rewards

We've reached the point where your doubt and uncertainty should be behind you and you should have clear and meaningful goals in front of you. Now your talent and innate genius will be free to soar. Before you know it, you'll be as involved in what you're doing as any star athlete, great scientist, famous artist, financial wizard, religious leader, or successful land baron who ever lived. You should be ready, right now, to face and enjoy "the best years of your life."

At this point, you might be thinking, "Maybe I set my goals too high. After all, I'm retired. I want to have some fun while I'm working toward my goals."

Good! That's another characteristic of highly successful people. They're able to reward themselves for progress, no matter how slight. They recognize that every step forward is a step toward greater satisfaction, and they reward themselves all along their journey. That's why we had you include some mental goals, spiritual goals, and physical goals, along with your personal and professional goals. However, the reward you give yourself doesn't even have to be related to any of the goals.

R. Frances Stern, a psychologist who works with burned out people who are suffering stress, emphasizes we need to get high on ourselves. Stern feels that good, hard, honest work must be rewarded if it's going to be repeated. And if you keep doing what you do best, you're bound to be successful.

Work becomes play when you enjoy it so much you'd do it even if you weren't getting paid for it. That's one of the keys to these five steps. Enjoy your work and have fun. When you reach this level, if you care enough and work hard enough for the result, you'll attain it. In other words, if you want to be rich, you will be rich. If you want to be successful in your field of endeavor, you will be successful. You can accomplish almost anything if you try hard enough.

Let others make you feel good, too. Nothing is as demeaning as false modesty. When you do something good, other people will want to tell you you are great. Let them. Don't be like the people who reject compliments and ignore kind words. If you do that long enough, you'll begin to believe it and stop believing you've really done something good. Then you'll stop trying, and that would certainly be a grave mistake.

When other people tell you you've done a good job, say, "Thank you. I really appreciate hearing it from you." You deserve their compliments—and they deserve the opportunity to compliment you on a job well done.

There will be times when you'll do something fantastic and there won't be anyone around to see you do it. That's too bad, but what the heck. Reward yourself anyway. Pat yourself on the back. Buy yourself an ice cream cone and tell yourself how great it is to be you and how wonderful it is to have and to achieve significant goals. No one can be better at giving praise or deserve it more than you.

Sometimes you're going to have to walk away from your work, no matter how much fun you're having. That will happen whether you think you need it or not. There are three reasons for giving yourself some quality time away from your work. They are your health, your need for mental freshness, and the happiness of your loved ones. These, by the way, are some of the factors Dr. Machlowitz found to be associated with the happy people she called "workaholics."

You've got to know when to stop and smell the flowers if you want to stay healthy, keep the creative juices flowing, and ensure the continued support and love of your family. That's as important as needing to know when to dive into your work to make things happen again. This means you must have some self-control. You must have enough self-control to stop working when the need arises and enough self-control to make yourself go back to work after you've rejuvenated your mind and body.

Take Care of Your Health

We've mentioned before that retirees are healthier than people their same age who have not retired. This often relates to the fact retirees are, for the most part, relieved from the stress of working at a job they don't like. But retirees must keep active mentally and physically or their health will deteriorate.

We've also pointed to the fact that successful people are healthy people. They feel good about themselves psychologically, and they don't suffer from anxiety and stress when they do the things they want to do and are good at. That's because successful people have a great sense of self-esteem and they believe in the things they're doing. They also take care of their bodies. They eat right to keep trim. They exercise to keep fit, and they work to stay in good health.

Have you observed what other retirees are doing to keep fit? They're swimming. They're walking at the malls. They're playing golf and tennis and handball. They're doing isometrics and calisthenics. They're cycling. The best exercises are rhythmic, continuous, and vigorous. The best exercises are those that stimulate the heart, blood vessels, and lungs without overtaxing you. Particularly recommended are brisk walking, swimming, rope skipping, and cycling. Most people over 60 avoid jogging, running, and other more strenuous sports activities.

We live this life a heartbeat at a time. That's why it's so important to keep your heart strong with reasonable and sensible exercise. After I exercise, I've found things just seem to fall into place. I conceptualize more clearly. My big problems seem to have diminished in size, and it's amazing how much faster I complete whatever task I've been working on.

Look around you at the successful people in your life. I'll bet you find most of them have some sort of body fitness program or simple exercise scheduled into their lives. They enjoy their leisure, and they go all out at having fun. But they also know that to enjoy their leisure and still meet their goals and dreams, they have to be physically and mentally fit. They work hard, and they play hard. And you should do the same. You should take the time to preserve the machine that holds and nourishes your spirit and fuels your fun. When it works well, you'll work well.

So take yourself off the bottom of the list of people to be taken care of. Now's the time you can set your own schedule. Be sure you have some exercise and fun scheduled into your daily itinerary and goals. If you have been sedentary, more activity is needed. Quality time for yourself is something you deserve after all those years of work. Let go of yourself. You can afford it. These are "the best years of your life."

Live Longer

A sound body and mind are an advantage for everyone, but you need something else. This was pointed out to me by my daughter, Libby, now in medical school and on her way to becoming a doctor. She found an article in the Boston Globe in which a psychologist, Peter L. Brill, emphasizes the importance of being in the right job. Now isn't that what I've been telling you all along? Dr. Brill pointed out that the key to personal self-esteem and well-being is a sense of competency.

He concluded that working at the right job was more conducive to longevity than diet, exercise, or heredity. So if you're working at the right job or retirement activity, living by the Five Steps to the Best Years of Your Life, and taking care of yourself, you should have a longer life than Methuselah.

Stay Mentally Fresh

No matter how well you're doing what you want to do, you can do it better by exposing yourself to interests and ideas outside your immediate day-to-day activities. It works like this. The ideas, problems, and solutions you encounter will spark your imagination and give you ideas you can use in your own work. This phenomenon is called "problem solving by analogy" by those who study problem solving and decision making.

A few vignettes from history will support this. For example, the first hot air balloon was designed by the LaGoffiere brothers after they saw bits of charred paper floating up their chimney. Leonardo da Vinci and the Wright brothers got their ideas about airplanes after watching birds in flight. Newton supposedly developed the laws of gravity after he saw an apple fall.

We're told one thing that actually improves as we grow older is our power to conceptualize. The key to problem solving by analogy lies in seeing something work in an environment that is foreign to the one you're working in and then asking "what if" questions. Many of the things medical scientists know about the human body were learned by asking "what if" questions. "What if blood flows through the body like water in the aqueducts of Rome?" asked Marcello Malpighi, the Italian physician who eventually discovered the vessels and arteries of the circulation system. "What if the nervous system acts like a telephone switchboard?" asked someone else. "And what if the brain works like a computer?" wondered another.

Look at the things that surround you and the way other people do things. You too will make many discoveries. They might not be earth-shaking, but they will help you.

If you get into the habit of asking "what if," as you're exposed to situations and things that are new to you, you'll find a whole new world opening up to you. It's fun to take things that you see and adapt them to your own needs.

Have you ever noticed the way your mind works? It's a wonderful problem solver, but sometimes it gets overloaded. It quits working on tough problems and goes on to do something else. You start thinking about something totally different. In effect, this gives your mind a rest—even though your subconscious mind might still be working on the most important problem. Suddenly an answer comes to you! It's like a light has been turned on, and you see the solution to the big problem.

I sometimes wake up at night because a great idea for something new or a solution to a problem has popped into my mind. When that happens I'm wide awake. I've found the best thing to do is to write it down and then go back to sleep. Without writing it down, I'd never go back to sleep. I get some good ideas that way, but I must confess some of those brilliant ideas that come to me at 3 a.m. don't look so brilliant in the light of day.

I've never failed to get at least one, and sometimes several, wonderfully creative ideas when I'm on vacation. Of course, now that I'm retired, I spend two months in Florida each winter. It's planned into my schedule. I feel I'm entitled to it. It always takes a few days to unwind after I get there—to forget the phone calls I should have made and the letters I should have written. Once that's behind me, I'm in deep, rich, creative pay dirt.

The time you spend to explore your mind is not time spent goofing off. It's productive time. You expose yourself to quality diversions that refresh and enrich your thoughts. You should pursue these thoughts every day.

Also, you should keep a record of your thoughts and conclusions, whether it's handwritten, typed, or recorded on cassette tape. You should broaden your view of the world and extend your areas of interest beyond your work.

Get your head out of the sand and think about, read about, and concentrate on something other than your work, regardless of how much pleasure your work is giving you. You can be more creative, productive, and efficient by expanding your horizons. Do it, and you'll find variety is the spice of success and the key to enjoyment in every aspect of your life.

Spend Time with Your Family

Time with your family tends to keep your life in proper perspective. Of course you don't have any little ones at home anymore, but if you're lucky, your family has multiplied. Your children have married, and now you have grandchildren. And, with or without grandchildren, there's always your spouse or friends and relatives, loving and supporting you.

One of the most critical elements in our lives is loving and being loved. As important as your work might be for you, it's only a tiny insignificant twitch in the universe we live in, compared with the love you should give to your family and can receive from them.

So no matter how good you want to become or how much you want to achieve, it'll be a hollow victory without the good will and love of those who are close to you. You might win the battle if you spend all your time working. But it will be at the cost of everything worth striving for if you don't spend time with your family and nurture that love they have for you.

Success cannot come at the expense of the people you love. Take a look at your family life now to be sure it's not marred by the tension of expecting the impossible and by constant quarreling, scolding, and fault finding. If things in your home aren't exactly as you expected them to be in your retirement, just remember it takes two to tango. Maybe you need to adapt to a life-style that has been in place there through all of your working years.

As joyful as your work is and as important as your achievements may be, they'll never be enough on their own to completely sustain you. Your loved ones might not be interested in your work, or they might not understand what it is that you do. But that shouldn't keep you from making a special place for them in your life.

You only go around once in a lifetime, so you want all the gusto you can get. Just be sure to take the loved ones along. Without them, it's not a trip, it's a stumble.

Write It Down

We're reaching the end of this step and the end of this book. The chapter has been short and sweet. I've tried to make it very logical and easy to read, just as it should be. You've done the first four steps with all your ability and all your enthusiasm. You deserve something that's simple and direct.

Again, we've added some worksheets at the end of this chapter. Please don't make the mistake of skipping over them too quickly or not concentrating on them. Rewards and positive reinforcement are very necessary ingredients in any forward progress toward success.

Spend some quality time concentrating on the fun you'll enjoy in each of the major areas of your life. Then write them down on the next two pages and refer to them religiously—as you will do with the previous exercises.

Don't forget to include your family in the fun.

If I've done the first four steps correctly, I deserve to have fun . . . and I will!!

Notes on Having Fun

What I Anticipate Enjoying

Personal enjoyment

Professional enjoyment

Mental enjoyment

Physical enjoyment

Spiritual enjoyment

Additional Notes to Myself

The Best Years of Your Life

Well, my friend, you've reached the best years of your life. You have the maturity and the experience you need to make whatever decisions are necessary for the best years of your life.

We've traveled through each page of this book together. That in itself means you are a person who, like myself, is dedicated to maximizing your God-given talents. It means you're really serious about this challenge to do something with these best years. It means you won't be one of those retirees who just sits in front of the TV and wastes away.

I don't know what goals you have set for yourself. I don't know whether you've decided to start your own business, get a part-time job, travel around the world, or donate your time to your favorite civic enterprise. What I do know is if you have used this book as it was designed to be used, you're a lot better prepared for these best years than you were before you started to read the book.

We've separated ourselves from the window shoppers and tire kickers, who are forever looking and talking but don't have the guts or commitment to do the necessary things we've done in this book. Remember this is a living thing. It doesn't stop here. You have the daily goals and the weekly goals and the monthly goals and the yearly goals to refer to from time to time and update.

What You See is What You Get

As you crank up your sights and prepare to shoot for the moon, please keep this in mind. "What you see is what you get." Remember, success is an "inside job." It's inside your own mind.

If you see a successful and productive retirement life, that's what you'll get. If you see mediocrity or failure in retirement, that's what you'll get. You've got the ammunition right now to give you what you want in the best years of your life. You've written goals for success in whatever endeavor you plan during those years. I've never seen anyone set goals for becoming a failure.

So you've chosen the target area. Set your sights on it. Be sure you're on target. You have to cleanse your mind and expectations of any thoughts of failure—of any remembrances of past disappointments or low esteem. If you're on target with the goals you set, you can do it! You can whip the world if you want to.

If you've taken the contents and suggestions of this book seriously and completed the exercises, then you're on your way to a happy future. You're consciously and subconsciously expecting success.

Each and every one of us has in our minds a giant television screen that operates 24 hours a day. It runs in the midst of activity, in quiet times, and while we're asleep. A soap opera plays on that screen, and we're the stars. How we picture ourselves on that screen is exactly how we're going to end up our lives. It's our own self-image that we picture there. What you see is what you get. We'll be no richer, no poorer, no happier, no sadder than how we picture ourselves in our own self-image.

You have written the script for your own real life play. In order to make the " best years of your life" everything you want them to be, you have to follow the script. Your goals and your dreams are there. You've broken the big script down into easy to follow, day-to-day steps. Throw yourself into it. Dress rehearsals start now. You'll have to refer regularly to your daily, weekly, and monthly scripts, and you might have to make some changes to the script. But these will be running changes—as the play goes on.

Remember that a mind, once expanded by thought, never shrinks back to it's original size. My fondest wish is that the thoughts and ideas we've shared in this book will expand your hopes and desires and truly make your retirement years the best years of your life. I hope the *Five Steps to the Best Years of Your Life* will help you achieve the successful retirement you've planned and deserve—a life that's productive and full of satisfaction, contentment, and joy. I hope you're like Peanuts of Charlie Brown fame, who, when asked what he wanted to be when he grew up, said, *"I want to be incredibly happy."*

INDEX

Social Security Administration, 6
Stern, R. Frances, 117

T
Terkel, Studs, 89
Tesar, Charles, 92
Thoreau, 42
Twin Cities Magazine, 92

U
United Packinghouse Workers of America, 89
United States Government, 47

W
Wall Street, 47, 49, 95
Washington, Booker T., 91
West, Mae, 42
Wilcox, Ella Wheeler, 61
Winds of Fate, The, 62
Wright Brothers, 121

Y
Y-Uncles, 30, 31

If you found this book helpful and would like more information on this and other related subjects, you may be interested in one or more of the following titles from our *Wellness and Nutrition Library.*

BOOKS
Diabetes 101: A Pure and Simple Guide for People Who Use Insulin (110 pages)
Expresslane Diet: (176 pages)
Retirement: New Beginnings, New Challenges, New Successes (140 pages)
Whole Parent/Whole Child: Raising a Child with A Chronic Illness (175 pages)
Diabetes: A Guide to Living Well (365 pages)
D.A.S.H. Diabetes. . . Actively Staying Healthy (160 pages)
Adult Braces in a Gourmet World (148 pages)
I Can Cope: Staying Healthy With Cancer (202 pages)
Managing Type II Diabetes (148 pages)
Managing the School Age Child With a Chronic Health Condition (350 pages)
Pass the Pepper Please (66 pages)
The Guiltless Gourmet (170 pages)
The Joy of Snacks (270 pages)
Fast Food Facts (56 pages)
Convenience Food Facts (188 pages)
Learning to Live Well With Diabetes (392 pages)
The Physician Within (170 pages)
Exchanges for All Occasions (250 pages)
Opening the Door to Good Nutrition (186 pages)

BOOKLETS & PAMPHLETS
Eating With Food Choices (40 pages)
A Guide to Healthy Eating (60 pages)
Diabetes & Alcohol (4 pages)
Diabetes & Exercise (20 pages)
Emotional Adjustment to Diabetes (16 pages)
A Step in Time: Diabetes Foot Care (18 pages)
Diabetes Record Book (68 pages)
Diabetes & Brief Illness (8 pages)
Diabetes & Impotence: A Concern for Couples (6 pages)
Adding Fiber to Your Diet (10 pages)
Gestational Diabetes: Guidelines for a Safe Pregnancy and Healthy Baby (24 pages)
Recognizing and Treating Insulin Reactions (4 pages)
Hypoglycemia (functional) (4 pages)

PROFESSIONAL SERIES

Manual of Clinical Nutrition (540 pages)
Simplified Learning Series—17 booklet preview packet
Diabetes Youth Curriculum: For working with young
people with diabetes, ages 6 to 16

The *Wellness and Nutrition Library* is published by Diabetes Center, Inc., in Minneapolis, Minnesota, punblishers of quality education materials dealing with health, wellness, nutrition, diabetes, and other chronic illnesses. All our books and materials are available nationwide and in Canada through leading bookstores. If you are unable to find or books in your favorite bookstore, contact us directly for a free catalog.

DCI Publishing, Inc.
P.O. Box 739